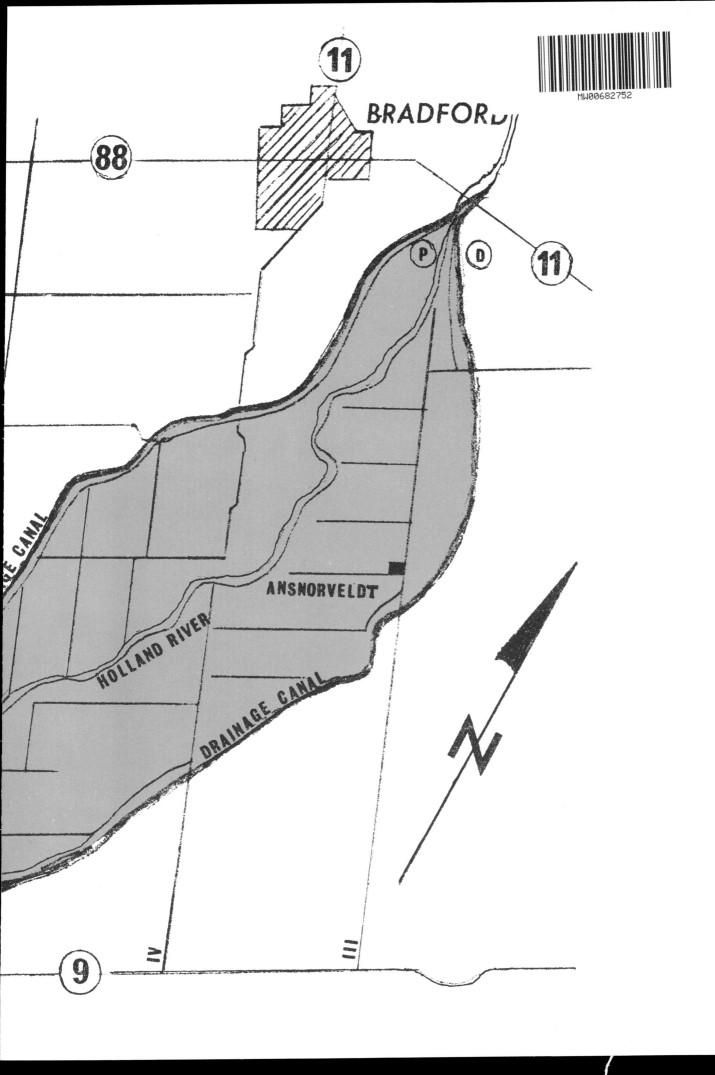

BRADFORD

ANSNORVELDT

HOLLAND RIVER

DRAINAGE CANAL

CANAL

AND THE SWAMP FLOURISHED

And the Swamp FLOURISHED

The Bittersweet Story of Holland Marsh

Albert VanderMey

VANDERHEIDE PUBLISHING CO. LTD.
Surrey, B.C., Canada - Lynden, WA, USA

And the Swamp Flourished

The Bittersweet Story of Holland Marsh

by Albert VanderMey
Copyright © Vanderheide Publishing Co. Ltd., 1994
All rights reserved.

Typesetting by Karin van der Heide
Cover design by Detmer K. Deddens
Layout by DK Designer Graphics
Edited by Martin P. van Driel
Published by Vanderheide Publishing Co. Ltd.
P.O. Bag 9033, Surrey, British Columbia V3T 4X3 Canada or
P.O. Box 313, Lynden, Washington 98264-0313 USA.
Printed in Canada.

VanderMey, Albert
And the Swamp Flourished
The Bittersweet Story of Holland Marsh

Includes bibliographical references and index.
ISBN 1-895815-01-0

1. Holland Marsh (Ont.) -- History
2. Dutch Canadians -- Ontario -- Holland Marsh -- History.
I. Title.
FC3095.H64V35 1993   971.3'547   C93-091867-3
F1059.H64V35 1993

Acknowledgements

Many of the photographs in this book were taken by Wayne Roper, an award-winning news photographer and co-author of Weekend Miracle (Boston Mills Press, 1986) and Travel Ontario (Boston Mills Press, 1987). Art Janse, the drainage superintendent of the Marsh, also made available a generous selection of his photographic work. We are also indebted to the Ontario Ministry of Agriculture and Food, the Archives of Ontario, the Scott Library at York University, the Toronto Star Syndicate, the Ontario Heritage Foundation, the National Geographic Magazine, the National Museum of Canada and the Ontario Historical Society for supplying us with illustrative material. But the bulk of the pictures came from the private albums of many of the people mentioned between these covers, and we are very appreciative of the excellent co-operation, the offers of assistance and the hospitality which they extended to us.

Table of Contents

Dedication

The Dutch presence in North America began in 1609 when English navigator Henry Hudson, employed by the Dutch East India Company, chanced upon the Hudson River Valley while trying to find a new passage to Asia with his ship *De Halve Maen* (The Half Moon). The Netherlands, then an important seafaring nation, established sovereignty over the territory, calling it *Nieuw Nederland* (New Netherland), and regularly sent trading vessels there. The furs offered by native trappers found a ready and lucrative market in Europe.

After the formation of the Dutch West India Company, limited colonization of the region, including Manhattan Island, was begun. The ship *Nieuw Nederland* served as the vanguard, ferrying thirty families to the distant shores in 1624.

The numerically superior English eventually took over control of *Nieuw Amsterdam* (now New York City) and the other territory which the Netherlands had claimed and governed. But the Dutch inhabitants stayed, carrying on their lives and occupations as before, and continued to make a significant contribution to the development of what would become the United States of America.

For more than a century after the changeover, Dutch settlement in the New World was restricted almost exclusively to the former New Netherland. It was not until the American Revolution that a number of Dutch families headed north, to the Maritimes and Upper Canada, as Loyalists to the British Crown. But when emigration from the Netherlands increased rapidly in the mid-1800's, it was the United States, not Canada, that was the destination of choice.

The picture changed dramatically in the early 1890's when the opportunities afforded by the opening of the vast Canadian West to homesteaders caught the attention of people in the economically depressed farming communities in the northern part of the Netherlands. Under the Free Land Homestead Act of 1872, a settler could gain ownership of a quarter-section of unoccupied public land by meeting certain requirements, notably the construction of a dwelling and the clearing and breaking up of the ground for agricultural use.

The Netherlands-based Christian Emigration Society was the main proponent of locating Netherlanders on homesteads, viewing settlement in the Canadian West as a viable alternative to unemployment. It set out on a recruiting drive in the rural areas of the province of Friesland where many farm labourers, particularly hard hit by bad economic conditions, were harbouring thoughts of leaving the country.

In the spring of 1893 - now a century ago - the emigration society sent out 102 emigrants to Winnipeg, the capital of Manitoba, and Yorkton, a railway town 280 miles to the northwest, in Saskatchewan. In terms of numbers, this migration was insignificant; other European countries were much better represented in the settlement scheme. But this small group made history, launching the organized migration of the Dutch to Canada. Many others would follow in their footsteps, including some who had lived in Dutch settlements in the U.S.

For many, homesteading was extremely difficult, bringing profound disappointments. Some gave up on the pioneering way of life to try their luck in the urban centres. In Winnipeg, a number of Dutchmen saw an opportunity to earn a dollar by peddling fresh vegetables door to door. In time, encouraged by decent profits, a number began to explore the possibility of growing their own produce on rented acreage. By 1905, the Dutch had gained a reputation for producing vegetables of excellent quality.

Klaas de Jong, one of the arrivals of 1893, also became a market gardener after a stint in the service of the railway, and eventually earned the informal title of Cauliflower King of America. That came in 1926, after he had won the cup offered by the Forbes Seed Company for the best cauliflower shown in Cleveland, Ohio.

It was also in the 1920's that the next big migration from the Netherlands took place. Farm, construction and industrial labourers were in demand across Canada, and they arrived by the thousands. Among them were the men, women and children who would establish the Dutch community in another market gardening district: Ontario's Holland Marsh.

But the biggest wave came after the Second World War as tens of thousands of agriculturalists, and later skilled and professional workers as well, bade farewell to their war-ravaged homeland.

According to figures from the 1991 Canadian census, nearly one million Canadians are of Dutch descent. Sixty-three per cent of these also identified one or more other cultures or countries where they have roots. This still leaves over 358,000 Canadians of solely Dutch origin, forming the ninth largest ethnic group in the country.

The Dutch in Canada have built up an excellent reputation as solid citizens - knowledgeable, hard-working, dedicated, principled and proud - which is demonstrated in the story that you are about to read. It is to all these people that we dedicate this book in commemoration of the 100th anniversary of the start of organized migration from the Netherlands to Canada.

~~~

Introduction

The sun shone brightly in Holland Marsh, Canada's celebrated market garden, on a Saturday morning in early June of 1976. Its sharp rays accentuated the lushness of all the greenery that was sprouting from the black organic soil. Even an inexperienced eye could see that another excellent crop was in the making.

It was a perfect day for the market gardeners to be outside, in their fields. There was always much work to be done during the growing season.

Later in the day, however, some of the men replaced their workclothes with more formal wear and, accompanied by their spouses, headed for the old schoolhouse in Ansnorveldt, a hamlet built by Dutch immigrants. An important ceremony was at hand.

John van Dyke, who had lived in the Marsh since 1934, stepped onto the seat of a picnic table, took a moment to steady himself, and then began to read from prepared notes.

"It was about this time of the season, now forty-two years ago," he said, "that a small group of Dutchmen made preparations to move in here to build their little homes and to make a start at developing a small area of this seven thousand acres of swamp. At that time, one could call this area the middle of nowhere. No road to get here - just a road allowance."

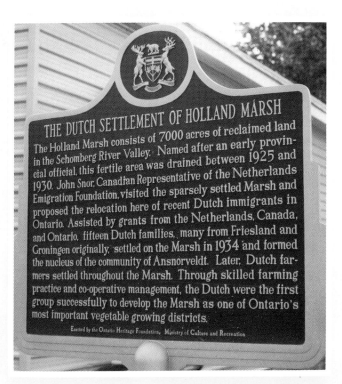

The historical plaque in Ansnorveldt.

His audience, including a number of government officials, listened with intense interest. Some of them were hearing the story for the first time.

"Somehow the lumber for the dwellings got here," Van Dyke continued, "and the men got busy nailing their future homes together. These were nothing but a shell - a roof over their heads. But what could one expect? They were allowed to spend only $200 on them, and even in the Depression years, a home could not be built and completely finished for $200. In September of that year, the families could move in, and for most of them it was the first home that they could really call their own. But to permanently live on this barren, flat marsh was not easy. Since money was a scarce commodity, everyone had to resort to the use of old tree roots to cook and to keep warm. They were quite plentiful. The soil was full of them in this neighbourhood. The modern conveniences as we know them today were, of course, totally absent. It was pioneering all the way."

On Van Dyke's left stood a plaque erected by the Ontario Heritage Foundation, an agency of the Ministry of Culture and Recreation. A mauve cloth hid the inscription.

"To work the land was hard slugging. A few small garden tools were the only things they had to cultivate their plots. The whole family had to pitch in to keep the weeds down and get the crop off in time. Many mistakes were made before they planted the right varieties of seed at the right time. There were no research people to whom they could turn for advice; they were completely on their own. Many meetings were held by the

John van Dyke: "It was hard slugging."

Invited guests pose with original settlers Mr. and Mrs. Marinus van Dyken (with hats) after the plague unveiling.

men of the settlement to find ways and means of obtaining the seed varieties and fertilizers best suited for this type of soil. Mostly it was just guesswork, resulting in some success and some failure and in the end a very small return for their hard work. This sometimes led them to get discouraged and to wonder whether coming out here to live under such difficult circumstances was worth it all."

Also present were Marinus van Dyken and his wife who, like Van Dyke, counted themselves among the original settlers of Ansnorveldt. Walter Horlings, another early arrival in the Marsh, was there too. They knew all about the hardships.

"The strong community spirit kept them at it. That made them stand together shoulder to shoulder in moments of disappointment and, come what may, to stick it out. This spirit was the secret of their determined attitude. Secondly, when the little homes were built and family life was established, they did not forget to also look after the spiritual needs. They strongly believed that where it was their duty to till the soil, there was One

greater than they who would have to give sun and rain for growth, and in time also the harvest. They built a very small church where they would gather on Sundays to seek encouragement and strength to carry on in the task for the week ahead. Here I think lay their strength and faith to carry on in the future..."

More people spoke. Then it was time for the unveiling by Horlings, an esteemed resident.

As the cloth was pulled away, the onlookers inched forward to read the wording below the heading The Dutch Settlement of Holland Marsh. The brief historical description ended with this sentence: "Through skilled farming practice and co-operative management, the Dutch were the first group successfully to develop the Marsh as one of Ontario's most important vegetable-growing districts."

There were handshakes all around. It was a day of honour for the Dutch.

What follows is their remarkable story.

~~~

The Promised Land

"A mere ditch swarming with bullfrogs and water snakes."

John Galt, one of the mainstays of the Canada Company, a venture which opened up former Crown land for settlement, obviously wasn't too impressed with his surroundings when he stopped in 1825 at a marshy expanse some thirty miles due north of Toronto in the Canadian province of Ontario, then called Upper Canada. True, it was not an ideal spot for carrying out a colonization scheme. Settlers needed arable land, not a swamp, to have a decent chance at survival.

As he stood on the highlands, looking down across the valley, the Scottish-born novelist could barely discern the meandering river. It was surrounded by marsh reeds, bulrushes and semi-aquatic flowers. Farther away from the water course was swampland, and beyond that hardwood bush. No, this wasn't an area that could be readily developed into a settlement, especially since it evidently was prone to flooding. Unimpressed, Galt moved on.

A few decades earlier - in 1791 to be exact - a Dutch-born surveyor and cartographer named Samuel Johannes Holland had visited the area during a general survey of the Lake Simcoe region. At that time, he was Surveyor-General of the province of Quebec and the northern district of North America, quite an important position in the new territory.

This man would lend his name to the marshland, which stretched southwesterly from Cook's Bay at the southernmost tip of Lake Simcoe to near the village of Schomberg, an extreme length of nearly twenty miles. The river and its branches would also be named after him, as would a nearby settlement, Holland Landing, the end of the portage leading to Lake Simcoe and Georgian Bay and the site of distribution of Indian presents and treaty payments.

Major Holland, born in 1728 near Nijmegen, also must have been unmoved as he regarded the wasteland that spread before him. Sure, it looked serene, even pretty. But it was a useless stretch - except of course, to the countless ducks, geese, pheasants, partridges, deer, rabbits and other forms of wildlife which flourished in the water and among the dense growth.

Little did Holland, a former soldier in the Dutch and British armies, realize that the area he was putting on the map would one day, more than 140 years later, be settled and developed by people from the country he had left far behind in his search for adventure and advancement.

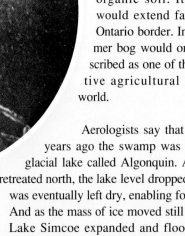

Samuel Johannes Holland

At first, the name was applied to the entire tract of marsh, some twenty thousand acres in total. Later, only the area which had been diked and pumped dry and worked by the Dutch and others would carry the designation.

Holland Marsh would become renowned for the quality of the vegetables grown in its organic soil. Its reputation would extend far beyond the Ontario border. In fact, the former bog would one day be described as one of the most lucrative agricultural areas in the world.

Aerologists say that thousands of years ago the swamp was covered by a glacial lake called Algonquin. As the glacier retreated north, the lake level dropped and the area was eventually left dry, enabling forests to grow. And as the mass of ice moved still farther north, Lake Simcoe expanded and flooded south of Cook's Bay, causing a swamp to form.

John Galt

The trees died and fell. Mosses grew, and so did a variety of other plants, including reeds, sedges, cattails, bulrushes and shrubs. These gradually decomposed. But they accumulated faster than the natural processes of decay were able to proceed, resulting in organic matter being built up layer after layer.

This vast, fibrous sponge of peat, commonly referred to as muck, varied in depth from a few inches to as much as forty feet and extended on both sides of the Holland River to a total width of between one and a half to two miles.

This type of organic soil isn't rare in Canada. Some estimates have put the total area at half a million square miles. But in the early days, with so much other land around, few people even considered reclaiming marshes for agriculture production. Nowadays, there's a concerted drive to preserve the remaining untouched areas in their natural state, thus leaving a bit of the original Canada for the benefit of wildlife and the enjoyment of generations to come.

When Major Holland visited the swamp south of Cook's Bay, the only inhabitants in the immediate area were Indians, who knew they could do business with the white men at the end of the portage. It was not until the early 1800's that a scat-tering of settlers came to the wooded hills overlooking the valley. Three Irishmen crossed the Holland River in 1819 and built a cabin in the area. Soon after them came a party of Scottish colonists who had made the long, arduous journey from the trouble-ridden Selkirk settlement on the Red River, in what is now the neighbouring province of Manitoba, in their search for the promised land.

In 1829, a few years after Galt's dismissal of the valley as a "mere ditch," more activity took place on the northern highlands; a man named William Milloy built a log tavern at the fork of a road leading from the Scotch settlement. A year or two later, a surveyor laid out a number of streets. The present town of Bradford was in the making.

The settlers, including the original Scots, felt themselves isolated to a large extent by a stretch of marsh to the east. In effect, they were cut off from Holland Landing, still an important place then with its direct link to Toronto. They petitioned the government and local authorities for help. This paid off; grants enabled them to build a corduroy road - one made from logs - over the swampland. A floating bridge got them across the river. Another stretch of logs completed the connection to the

This 1948 photo of a marshy area depicts how most of Holland Marsh looked prior to reclamation.

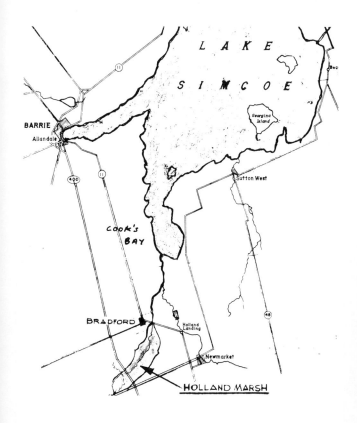

HOLLAND MARSH

Lake Simcoe, and thereby dropping the level of both lakes and the Holland River. This would provide an outlet for the drainage of the marshland. However, strenuous opposition from settlements on Lake Simcoe, whose shoreline property owners could foresee great damage, prevented such a scheme from moving beyond words and sketches.

The harvesting of the abundant marsh grass and reeds after 1880 was the first real industry on the marshland. The hay was much in demand in Toronto and other centres for stuffing mattresses. At first, strong hands and scythes were used. Later, horse-drawn mowers did most of the work.

A flat-bottomed scow ferried the horses across the flooded area. But the soggy ground wouldn't support them; they became hopelessly mired. The problem was solved by strapping rectangular boards to the hoofs. The horses then stepped along neatly, legs slightly apart, much like someone on snowshoes.

The hay business continued to grow, reaching its peak around 1915. By that time, hay was being cut on approximately twelve thousand acres.

A few years earlier, in 1910, an enterprising young farmer from the Scotch settlement, David Watson, who had set up a grocery business in Bradford, sparked renewed interest in reclamation. He was convinced that a large part of the valley to the south could be developed into agricultural land. Accordingly, he invited William Henry Day, professor of physics at the Ontario Agriculture College in Guelph, to do some soil testing at Holland Marsh and to ascertain whether a feasible plan could be worked out for draining it.

landing. Incidentally, during reconstruction in 1992 of what is now Highway 11 (Bridge Street), which included removing organic soil from beneath the roadbed, sections of the corduroy road were uncovered and removed.

A ways beyond the crossing, another town site was laid out in 1836. It was called Amsterdam, obviously as a further recognition of Major Holland's precursory efforts in opening up the region. As an added touch, the streets on the map were given Dutch and Flemish names such as De Ruyter, Van Dyke, De Wit and Rubens.

Unlike Bradford, Amsterdam did not grow at all. It remained largely a bush-covered tract. In 1869, a lumberman named Thompson Smith purchased the site and used it as the base for developing a prosperous lumber industry in the area. Other sawmills also sprang up, even on the Bradford side of the river, employing hundreds of men.

Not much remains of Amsterdam today. Most people don't even know it existed. There are a few oldtimers, however, who continue to refer to the area by its original name.

A number of the early settlers, having ventured onto the marshland, pondered ways of partially draining certain sections so that the peat could be extracted for fuel. A few others, not ready to discard the valley as a mere ditch, went so far as to break up some of the swamp for possible agricultural use. But it was too wet for cultivation, and the efforts were abandoned.

Even so, the idea of turning the bog into something useful persisted. The favoured plan of reclamation involved the lowering of the Washago outlet of Lake Couchiching, which adjoins

Professor William Day

The headquarters of the Thompson Smith lumbermill in Amsterdam.

Professor Day, born near Lindsay, Ontario, graduated from the University of Toronto in 1903 and was appointed head of physics at Guelph three years later. At that time, the college was running drainage surveys across the province, attempting to create a soil map "both of old and new Ontario, particularly new Ontario, so that the agricultural capabilities of new sections might be known beforehand without experimenting on the part of the settlers."

The professor carefully examined the marshland and the surrounding watershed and concluded, much to Watson's delight, that drainage was possible without having to lower the level of Lake Simcoe. Three basic steps would be necessary:

- A cut-off ditch or canal would have to be constructed around a large section of the swamp southwest of the Toronto-Barrie highway crossing just east of Bradford. This channel, along the base of the highlands, would prevent water from flowing onto the morass or into the old river course. The highland water, shut off from the river, would then be diverted along the canal which would empty into the river below the reclaimed area.

- A dam would have to be built across the river at the lower end of the reclaimed area, near the highway crossing, to prevent lake water from backing up into the enclosed portion of the old river bed.

- Pumps would have to be installed in a pumping plant to remove runoff water from the enclosed river section. With

the level maintained four to five feet below the soil surface, there would be ample outlet for drainage.

Later that year, Watson, still bubbling with enthusiasm, wrote the professor: "As I stood tonight at sunset and looked over our 'promised land' with its broad acres of unbroken greatness with the wooded hills of King Township in the background, I felt a glance of pride at the immense possibilities which lie in the scheme."

The professor, too, had become hooked on the possibilities. The following year, he had some produce - celery, potatoes, pumpkins, oats and beans - planted on the marshland that juts right up to Bradford. A small plot at the rear of Lukes' Mill had been heaped up a foot or two to render it dry. Day later reported: "All of the vegetables matured, the quality being excellent, the celery carrying off the prize at the local fall fair."

So satisfactory were the results that he and a number of associates formed a development syndicate which eventually purchased four thousand acres. Then he continued to advocate reclamation, saying the black muck, high in lime and medium in other mineral content, was almost identical in composition with the famous onion lands of Point Pelee, the strong sugar-beet area of Wallaceburg and the wonderful celery land of Thedford, all in Ontario, or the world-renowned celery soil of Kalamazoo, Michigan.

Contacts were made with local municipal officials to have the work carried out under the province's Municipal Drainage Act. Under its provisions, such a project could proceed provided at least two-thirds of the affected landowners would agree to it. The municipalities would guarantee debentures and assess the cost on an acreage basis.

However, nothing was resolved in the discussions, not even after a deputation pointed out that the land, assessed at less than $1 an acre, would jump to as high as $50 an acre if reclaimed. Enthusiasm for municipal involvement did not run high, the feeling being that the reclamation should be carried out by a private corporation and with private capital. Then the First World War came along, precluding any further action.

After the restoration of peace, an attempt to have the project undertaken with private funds failed. Then, in 1923, the professor resigned his post at Guelph, moved to Bradford and began an energetic campaign to interest the village, and the townships of King and West Gwillimbury - the river forms the boundary between them - in his dream. A petition was circulated, covering some 7,265 acres, and most of the landowners signed it. A four-day motor trip to reclamation works in western

Ontario was arranged for local councillors and others. Yes, the professor was finally making headway.

The councils of West Gwillimbury and Bradford passed bylaws in 1924 and 1925, approving the drainage scheme, and a petition was forwarded to the provincial government. King Township was reluctant to get involved and appealed. But it was forced, under the Drainage Act, to join up.

On April 16, 1925, a contract for the reclamation, in the amount of $137,000, was let to the Toronto firm of Cummins and Robinson. A large scow was brought to the site. And work at last was begun on turning the "mere ditch" into productive land.

William Day and his backers were tickled pink as they watched the heavy machinery at work, digging out a canal around the perimeter of a virtually flat terrain of swamp and bush a little more than seven thousand acres in size.

True, with a big investment in the land, they were gratified to see the work under way. They had visions of soon making

Once drained, the land could be cleared and made ready for agricultural use.

huge profits. But the professor had an additional reason for smiling: his persistence had paid off, putting him a step away from personal victory in his drawn-out battle with the skeptics.

According to plans drawn up by engineer Alexander Baird of Sarnia, the canal would range in width from thirty-eight feet to seventy feet, have an average depth of seven feet and stretch 17 1/2 miles. The earth would be dumped on the marsh side, making a dike seven feet high and wide enough to support a road. Along the widest stretch of the canal, a smaller dike would be put on the outer edge with openings at intervals to admit water from the highlands.

A main dam would be built in the northeast corner, near the highway crossing, and smaller dams would be placed where the canal cut and diverted the north and west branches of the river. Two pumps, driven by electric motors, would be installed at the main dam.

The initial smiles gave way to frowns when the reclamation did not progress as quickly and smoothly as Day and the other landowners had hoped. There were numerous technical difficulties, including dike cave-ins and scow groundings. Lack of a co-ordinated plan and expert direction also caused delays and frustrations. In the end, Day and the others formed a landowners' association to lend some weight to their common concerns.

The professor was anxious to get agriculture under way and to get prospective land purchasers interested in the development.

He badly needed some income; his land acquisition had cost quite a bit. And the reclamation was bound to raise the assessment, and thus his taxes, even though the government had promised financial assistance under the Provincial Aid to Drainage Act after it had determined that the entire region stood to benefit.

A Dutch specialist in drainage was consulted. And so the work dragged on.

A much smaller scheme, with its own man-made drainage reservoir and encompassing some two hundred acres of prime land between Bradford and the diked area, grew its first crops in 1927. Known simply as the Bradford Marsh, it had been reclaimed separately, as the wording in the Drainage Act had prevented it from being included in the larger project.

Holland Marsh would not be completed until 1930. By that time, Canada and many other countries were already struggling under the terrible economic collapse known as the Great Depression.

Typically, Professor Day was bursting with optimism when he presented a progress report to the ratepayers of West Gwillimbury and King townships in December, 1930. He undoubtedly wanted to justify the expenditures, which an earlier calculation had put at $21 for each reclaimed acre. Still, he had some pretty convincing figures to back up his bright outlook.

During the past season, he said, he had thirty-seven acres under cultivation, growing head lettuce, celery, onions, carrots and parsnips. Other than the carrots and the parsnips, which were in cold storage, everything had been marketed. Cash receipts to date totalled $24,718, over and above the selling commission of 12 1/2 per cent. The carrots and parsnips, when sold, would bring the total to around $26,000, or an average yield of $702 an acre.

These were striking figures.

The professor singled out his lettuce crop for particular mention. Wholesale firms in Toronto had told him that never before had there been Canadian head lettuce on the Toronto market through the entire season. His lettuce appeared on July 11 and was on sale every day until October 11.

"We had two acres of lettuce maturing each week for eleven weeks," he said. "It was our largest crop, both in acreage and in returns, bringing us $11,867.78. We look forward to the time when Holland Marsh will supply the head lettuce for all Canada during the summer season, instead of its being imported from California, Arizona and other American states."

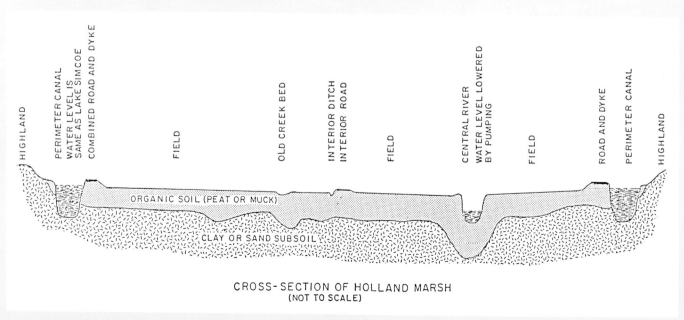

CROSS-SECTION OF HOLLAND MARSH
(NOT TO SCALE)

This sketch shows a cross-section of the Marsh.

The work gang hired by Professor Day for his gardening operation.

The muck of Holland Marsh holds moisture well at night and even cools the air a bit, allowing leafy plants such as lettuce to replenish the water they lose through evaporation during the day.

Actually, the professor's lettuce crop was not very good that year because of lingering drought. Many of the plants did not head properly. The solution, he explained, was more irrigation.

"Last summer, when we realized that a drought was on, we made a cut through the bank and let the water from the outside channel into our ditches. It spread out through them, and in a few days the soil, which had been dry and dusty on the surface, began to look moist as it became saturated with water. You see, the bottom of the ditches is about 2 1/2 feet below the lake level. That irrigation saved our celery from feeling the effects of the drought. But our inlet ditch was neither deep enough nor wide enough, and so the water never reached the lettuce fields farther down. For next year, we have two inlets, each admitting four times as much water as the old one."

He also pointed out the "sad part" of his farming operation: the abundant expenses. Mentioned were crates, baskets, bags, motor oil, garage and blacksmith costs, hired trucking, gasoline, fertilizer, cold storage and wages. The total nearly equalled half the value of the crop.

But the important thing was that the Marsh had proved its worth. A drainage commission - at first composed of the reeves and later broadened to include growers - looked after the pumping operations and the maintenance of the dike and the canal. This meant that the owners of the land could concentrate on breaking up more acreage and getting market gardeners to move in.

"Some people say we can't bring all this marsh under cultivation, for we'll glut the market," said Day. "At every stage of this project, from its inception to the present time, there has always been some wise one to rise in his wisdom and solemnly warn us: 'It can't be done.' But all difficulties to date have been safely negotiated, and this one will be too. The method of meeting

Tom Fuller

They did not think that the Marsh was good for anything but mattress hay. Professor Day proved them wrong. The carrot harvest is under way.

it has been in our minds for years. We'll have diversified crops, and canning and soup factories, and then see how easy it is. In the summer, we'll sell everything we can; what we can't, we'll can; then, in the winter, we'll sell all we can, and by spring be ready to start all over again."

He called the reclamation one of the biggest events to have occurred in Ontario in recent years. "Picture the hive of industry when the whole 7,500 acres is under cultivation and five thousand people are working daily on the Marsh and many others supplying their needs."

The skeptics weren't swayed by Day's glowing report. In fact, during the next few years, while the Depression ravaged even the lettuce market, their numbers grew. Nevertheless, the professor retained his admirers, including Tom Fuller.

As a spry nineteen-year-old, Fuller left his native England in 1927, ending up in Bradford, the adopted home of his older brother, Bill. He landed a job at the reclamation site; he had to dive under the dredges used in the canal work and undo bolts to dismantle them. After three months, he went to work at the Toronto Furniture Company on Holland Street, the village's main thoroughfare (Bradford did not gain town status until 1960). A few years later, when jobs became as scarce as hen's teeth, he began to work for Day in the fields at seventeen cents an hour.

"People didn't think the Marsh was good for anything except mattress hay," he recalled. "If you asked the average farmer outside the Marsh, the reply would be that it would never work. But Mr. Day knew it would work. I've never in my life seen a man so dedicated to his work as Mr. Day was."

~~~

The Dutch Arrive

In the summer of 1931, John Sytema and a friend, also a Dutchman, ran into car trouble while passing through Bradford on their way north to the Huntsville area to check over some real estate that was for sale. They had been told about a farm which included lakefront cottages and a dance hall. Sytema, young and eager, and with some experience in hotel management, had visions of delving into a profitable deal.

While the car was being repaired, the two young men decided to take a closer look at a tract of black soil near the road that had caught their eye. It was Professor Day's garden, covered with a blanket of lush vegetables.

"We had a good look at that soil and had a long talk with Professor Day," recalled Sytema, single then. "We were very impressed with what we saw and heard. If the property up north did not pan out, we intended to return to Bradford and look into the possibility of buying land there."

The farm in the vacation country did not live up to their expectations. The land was rocky and poor. Nor did they like the arrangement with the cottages, which included the preparation of meals for the occupants, something in which the two bachelors lacked skill. So back they went, somewhat disappointed.

But Sytema bubbled with enthusiasm when he reported his discovery of the Bradford and Holland marshes to his boss, Henry Poelman. Poelman rented a farm at Aldershot, a small community near Hamilton, then a drive of up to 2 1/2 hours

from the reclaimed area, depending on the route, the condition of the vehicle and the penchant of the driver to adhere to the low speed limits. They and another Dutchman, Peter Greyn, soon were headed for Day's domain, eager to inspect available land.

Back in 1927, while Holland Marsh was being made arable, the professor foresaw a need for Europeans to develop the land into productive allotments. He wrote: "Hollanders and Belgians make ideal market gardeners and the possibilities of this area for immigrants has already been brought to the attention of the immigration authorities of governments and railways, all of whom have shown active interest in the area with a view of placing its merits before these and other prospective or actual immigrants adapted to vegetable growing."

But the Europeans were slow in coming. A few Canadian-born farmers, inexperienced in working with muck, came on the scene. But many of the plots would soon be abandoned or taken for tax arrears. The depressed market conditions had compounded the many difficulties. Even Professor Day, involved as he was in complex land entanglements between his syndicate and the municipalities, must have been deeply discouraged at times that his dream of rapid development was not materializing.

The three Dutchmen from the Hamilton area were directed to the west end of the Marsh, just off the Town Line, now High-

John Sytema and Peter Greyn break up their land.

way 9. They trampled through dense weeds and undergrowth, carefully avoiding the sharp thistles and the pesky burrs. The terrain didn't look too inviting at this point; in fact, the soil wasn't even visible. With their feet, they pushed aside some of the growth and exposed the fibrous ground, the sight of which appealed to them immediately.

Before long, they had jointly purchased from Luke Gibbons a large chunk of unworked land, 175 acres in total, with one-eighth covered by bush. The price was reasonable: $35 an acre, with payment to start after the third year.

"In late fall, Peter Greyn and I went back to break up the land," recalled Sytema, who had acquired twenty-three acres in the deal, ten of which he later sold. "We had bought some machinery. Everything was still in a wild state. You can imagine that we felt like real pioneers. We ploughed up a lot of land, not without some difficulty. After that, we called it quits for the winter. We would return early in the spring to prepare the fields further and to put in the first crops."

During the winter, Sytema worked on a farm near Picton. He was in high spirits, despite some degree of apprehension over his financial commitment and the fact that he had little knowledge of market gardening and none at all of the peculiar requirements of the Marsh. But he was eager to learn, to experiment, to work long and hard. For him, the winter did not go quickly enough.

Encouraged by his friend who was already in Canada, Sytema had sailed for the New World in July, 1926. Twenty-two years old, just out of the army and with no steady job - there wasn't room for him in father's transportation business in Roordahuizum, in the northern Dutch province of Friesland - he had joined the growing legion of emigrants enticed by the promise of opportunities in Canada and elsewhere.

A farmer near Preston, Ontario, hired him for $30 a month, including room and board. Everything went fine. But a few months later, with winter around the corner, there was no more work. The friend, also jobless, headed for the West. Sytema stayed, struggled through the winter and then worked on a day-to-day basis until a disagreement forced him to hop aboard a westbound train also.

He eventually wound up as a night clerk at a forty-room hotel in Nelson, British Columbia. His limited English vocabulary didn't hinder him. But there came a time where he longed for other work. So he joined up with his friend and went to Vancouver, where they worked under contract as independent concessionaires for carnival operator Patty Conklin. They were in charge of the fish pond game of chance, paying a $60 fee at each place where the midway was assembled, and worked their way east as far as Winnipeg.

With the contract completed, and tired of the nomadic life, Sytema went back to the hotel in Nelson and was rehired as the night clerk. For two months, while the owner was visiting New York City, he was in complete charge of the place.

"After her return from New York, I worked for her for sixteen to eighteen months as hotel manager. Then I ran into health problems - fatigue. I had to get out of there. So I bought a one-way ticket to Holland and went back in March of 1931. Maybe,

just maybe, I would like it there. But I didn't. In August, I returned to Canada - via New York, as I had great difficulty getting a visa. At that time, because of the economic situation, Canada's door wasn't as open as it used to be. Poelman, my former boss, gave me a job."

In the spring of 1932, after the snow had melted and the robins had started returning from the warmer climes to the south, Sytema was in the Marsh to prepare his land for seeding. Greyn, who had emigrated in 1927 from Helden, in the southern province of Limburg, was there too. Poelman, the other partner, stayed at Aldershot, entrusting the care of his acreage to someone else.

The soil, still wet and dark, looked invitingly rich. Full of fervour, Sytema and Greyn tackled the remaining field work, used some guesswork in applying nutrients and then seeded the crops, mainly lettuce and carrots. After that, they had a full-time task keeping the rows clear of the flourishing weeds.

Sytema sits outside the hotel in British Columbia where he was the manager.

At the end of a long, arduous day, Sytema still had time left to drink in the splendour of his surroundings: the flat landscape, quite unlike anything he had seen in Ontario, the pungent soil, the nearby canal alive with wriggling polliwogs, the beautiful spring flowers, including the exquisite trillium among the trees in the bush...

He also observed that he and Greyn weren't alone in their neck of the Marsh. Immediately to the east was a farm operated by a Dutchman named Rol, who had been there for some time already. With three sons, this man rented land from Archie Saint, a lumber dealer in Bradford. His rental payments were waived on condition that ten acres be broken up each year. In the immediate area, there were also a number of Canadians tending to fields they either owned or rented.

In 1933, more Dutchmen arrived. Sytema recalled their names: Geytenberg, Koster, De Voght and Doormel. They worked forty acres in the extreme southwest corner of the Marsh under a deal arranged by John J. Snor, who had emigrated from the Dutch city of Utrecht in 1911, set up an antique furniture business in Hamilton and now was working on behalf of the *Stichting Landverhuizing Nederland* (the Netherlands Emigration Foundation) and some other interests, including a few of the landowners.

Snor, who would play a prominent role in the early development of the Marsh by inducing Dutch immigrants and others to start in business there, even had small, two-room cottages built along the perimeter where the new arrivals could spend the night. There were no houses yet on the Marsh. Even Sytema and Greyn, who had a family, lived in the highlands. The first real settlers, most of them Dutch, would not come until 1934. Snor, as we shall see, had a hand in that settlement as well.

"I don't think any of the ones who came shortly after us stayed very long," said Sytema. "A few more Dutchmen worked land north of us: De Vroom, Zweep, the Huitema brothers, and so on. But most of them didn't last either. They gave it a good, honest try. But it was rough in those days. After a year or two, many of them got discouraged and moved on. Greyn and I stuck it out."

There were times when Sytema thought of packing his bags too. Particularly disheartening was the development of a legal dispute over property boundaries. Snor, whose advice and assistance had been sought during the purchase, was now called upon to straighten out the entanglement.

"I can't say enough about Snor, who was an immensely proud man. Like Professor Day, he really believed in the viability of the Marsh. But he wasn't too sure yet of what could all grow nicely. In 1933, he asked me to grow flowers in a test plot. He supplied the fertilizer and the seed and paid me by the hour. Unfortunately, the flowers didn't amount to much and the test plot was abandoned."

Snor was a novice when it came to horticultural and agricultural matters. In the Netherlands, he had done some interior decorating, a line of work in which his parents were involved. Growing things was entirely foreign to him.

Nevertheless, he figured that the Marsh, with its peculiar soil, had great potential as a money-maker. And if there was money to be made, he wanted to be in on the action. That is why he experimented with flowers and even blueberries.

John Snor

Snor later moved to Bradford, as the antique business was a virtual bust during the Depression, but he never took up market gardening.

He did set up the Holland Bulb Company in Port Credit, near Toronto, after becoming acquainted with a Dutchman involved in the flower bulb business.

An obituary printed in a local newspaper after his death at close to seventy years stated: "Each spring it was Mr. Snor's policy to announce the time when the thousands of bulbs there were expected to be in full bloom and to open the breathtakingly colourful gardens to hosts of interested people."

Sytema sold his holdings in the Marsh in 1946 and moved his wife, Marie, and their children - they were expecting their fourth - to a fifty-acre farm at Pine Orchard, east of the neighbouring town of Newmarket. There he raised chickens and pigs and grew the odd commodity. In 1950, he went into the insurance business as well.

"When I first started working in the Marsh," he explained, "the people on the highlands said I was crazy. They couldn't figure out why anyone would put all his money and time into growing vegetables in a swamp. Well, something must have

Sytema (right) and a few other Dutchmen pose at a tractor that reared like a horse when something got caught in its axle.

caused them to change their opinion. When I pulled out, they said I was a fool. Many believed the Marsh was a place to make lots of money. That may have been true for some growers. But as for me, I didn't make much money. And all that hard work - without the modern tools that we have today - got to me. I couldn't wash behind my ears any more because of the rheumatism."

Sytema certainly stayed longer in the Marsh than most of the other early arrivals. And Greyn far outlasted him. There were others who merely put a foot inside and then left in a hurry, not particularly anxious to wade financially into what was then still an unknown quantity. Among such people were Peter Lugtigheid of the Chatham area, then a six to seven-hour drive away to the west, and Kees Spierenburg, who hailed from the Woodstock area, just three hours away.

"It was around 1932," recalled Lugtigheid. "I had been visiting Kees at his farm - he used to be a neighbour of mine in Holland - when we decided to check out the reports we had been hearing about Holland Marsh."

They rented a rowboat a couple of times to get around. They also made contact with Professor Day, who typically tried his utmost to convince them to relocate. He was particularly interested in the fact that Lugtigheid possessed around six hundred Dutch 'eenruiters', movable glass frames for greenhouses, which were employed as cold frames in getting vegetable plants off to an early start.

"We spent three or four days there," said Lugtigheid. "But we lost interest when we learned that there was a big legal dispute going on over the ownership of land. We didn't want to get mixed up with that."

Lugtigheid went back to Chatham and continued to develop a mixed farming operation with cattle, pigs and crops for canning. He nurtured no regrets. Son John eventually took over, looking after six hundred acres.

~~~

A New Beginning

In 1929, John van Dyke, a farm labourer in Friesland, was itching to emigrate to Canada. He was disgusted with the working conditions and discouraged over the bleak prospects for better times. Moreover, he didn't want to experience what his father had gone through.

"Dad was a worker on mixed farms, going from one place to another to eke out a living for a family of eight children. There was no such thing as a steady job. On his 25th wedding anniversary, he made a little speech, saying he had put his furniture on the wagon no fewer than fourteen times. This really prompted me to go to Canada. I did not want to go through the same thing myself."

In those days, the labourers spared no kind words for the gentleman farmers.

"Those farmers walked around with their fingers in their vests and just barked orders," recalled Van Dyke, born in the village of Hallum in 1906. "The workers didn't have a say in anything. They couldn't even make suggestions. No wonder they felt they were being treated no better than slaves."

Vivid in memory was his father rising at 3:30 in the morning to milk the cows. When this was done, there was a short

Van Dyke, as one of the original settlers of Holland Marsh, became the unofficial historian. He was always full of stories.

break for a few slices of bread. Then the man went back to work for another ten hours of hard work under the watchful eye of the boss.

"It was just a slave life. And my own experience wasn't much better. After our first son arrived, I told my wife: 'We have to get our of here now. Any place in the world is better than this. If we stay, how can we ever move ahead?'"

He confided his plans to his boss when he was called on the carpet following a rather heated argument during which the word bloodsucker was used.

"Some of my fellow workers had expected me to be fired. But when I mentioned to the farmer my strong desire to go to Canada, he became a different man. He thought it was a wonderful idea and that more people should be considering it. He even offered some help if we needed it, but I kindly declined."

To Van Dyke, Canada was not just an exotic word out of an atlas. His older brother, Albert, had moved there recently. According to the letters, Canada was not exactly a bed of roses either, but a much brighter future awaited the agricultural worker there. The message was clear: come over when you can.

Early in 1930, with all the formalities out of the way, Van Dyke booked passage for himself, wife Grace and son Bob on the *Nieuw Amsterdam*. It cost him $350, a princely sum in those days. The ship departed from Rotterdam on March 19. There were many other emigrants on board, including Van Dyke's oldest brother, Wopke, and his cousin, both with families.

They all felt relieved now that the big moment had arrived. The rough voyage across the storm-tossed ocean, and the misery of seasickness, did not lessen their anticipation of the better life that awaited them in the New World.

"We considered ourselves fortunate," remarked Van Dyke. "The Great Depression was on, and Canada wasn't too anxious to admit more immigrants, who might have to be supported by the state because of the increasing scarcity of jobs. We were among the last big groups allowed into Canada. Later, only those who had money would be admitted. So the door was pretty well closed."

The *Nieuw Amsterdam* docked at Halifax, on Canada's east coast, on March 27. A train brought the Van Dykes and some others to Hamilton two days later. Brother Albert, who lived in that area, was on hand to greet them. He gave brother John's hand an extra squeeze; it was the newcomer's 24th birthday.

Hamilton was one of the few areas in Ontario where Dutch immigrants had clustered. They had even set up their own church, of the Christian Reformed denomination, with Rev. John S. Balt, a home missionary, looking after the ministry. Naturally, newly-arrived immigrants were inclined to go to this region, despite attempts by some authorities to spread them out in favour of assimilation.

Another cluster, also with their own Protestant church, was to be found in the Chatham area, much farther to the west. Walter Horlings, who would become one of the pillars in the Marsh,

John van Dyke takes his son for a ride in the Hamilton area.

had arrived there in May, 1924, at the age of twenty-one. A representative of the Dominion Sugar Company had gone to Nieuwe Pekela, in the province of Groningen, where Horlings lived, to recruit workers for the sugarbeet farms. The rest of the large Harm Horlings family, except for the oldest son, would follow Walter to Chatham in stages.

"The ones already here sent money to Holland to pay for the fares," he explained. "As soon as we had a little left over, off to Holland it went. That's the only way we could get the whole family here."

In the Hamilton area, Van Dyke stayed with his brother for four weeks while he hunted high and low for a job.

"We didn't have a sponsor who would guarantee us work and a roof over our heads," he explained. "That system was set up for the next wave of immigrants, after the Second World War. There were no fieldmen to help us either. We were strictly on our own. Work was scarce, but I finally found a job with a farmer. After a short period there, I went to another farm, where I learned all about vegetable growing. Little did I know it then, but this experience would prove invaluable in the years ahead. All the farm jobs were seasonal, however, which meant that during the winter, with no other work around, I had to go on relief."

The food vouchers and the pay from the relief work carried the young family through those hard times, although barely. Many other people also suffered. But for recent newcomers, still not completely adjusted to the customs and the language, the blows seemed especially severe. Canada had not presented them with anything to rave about yet. And there were other hurdles to overcome: a struggle to get over initial misgivings, bouts of homesickness and periods of utter despondency and hopelessness.

To make matters worse, landed immigrants who were not naturalized citizens were in danger of being deported to their native countries if they continued to be a financial burden. This was not a hollow threat; almost thirty thousand immigrants would be forcibly returned over the course of the decade because of unemployment or illness.

Van Dyke was profoundly worried. He didn't want to go back to Holland, where the economic downturn had hit hard too. Despite all the difficulties, he had gotten to like Canada. Like many others in similar circumstances, he hoped the authorities would allow him to ride out the storm.

The Great Depression: unemployed workers hitch a ride on a freight train heading for Ottawa, Canada's capital, to demand jobs.

Dutch immigrants are on their way to church in Hamilton.

Then he heard about something that made him perk up his ears: an area called Holland Marsh, a few hours away by car, needed settlers, and the government was prepared to help a certain number of prospective ones on relief in relocating there.

John Snor, the representative of the Netherlands Emigration Foundation, also had been concerned about the deportation threat. But there was a way to avert that. Under the federal settlement scheme, many people on relief and in need of work were being put on land away from the urban centres. So why not Holland Marsh, where Snor had a close association with some of the major landowners?

In 1933, Snor and a Dutch official, J.A. Hartland, put the final touches on a plan to relocate families to the Marsh. Snor had arranged to have a 125-acre parcel of undeveloped land in

the eastern part, owned by the Canada Land Company, subdivided into twenty-five parcels of five acres each. These were laid out in strips parallel to the road allowance for the extension of Concession 3 of King Township. This land would be purchased by the settlers. The strip alongside the road allowance would be set aside for their houses, which they would have to build themselves.

The Horlings family belonged to the Christian Reformed Church at Chatham, where this picture was taken, and resettled later in Holland Marsh.

Abraham Havinga, one of the original settlers.

Each family would get $200 from the federal government, $200 from the provincial government and $200 from the Dutch government. Snor got the Netherlands involved when the local municipalities, originally part of the plan, failed to come up with their share, no doubt because of the lingering skepticism over the Marsh's worth.

"I remember the day the telegram came from Holland, confirming the participation," recalled Helen Sutton, one of Snor's three daughters. "Some people had gathered at our house, and tears of joy were streaming down their faces." .

There was a stipulation that the latter $200 portion had to be repaid over a period, but considerable doubt exists as to whether this occurred in all instances.

With this total grant of $600, the settlers could make a new beginning. Each would be allowed to spend $200 on the construction of his dwelling - a two-storey, frame structure measuring a mere sixteen feet by twenty feet. Another $200 could be spent on getting the five acres - this was considered a normal-size market garden in those days - ready for seeding and for the purchase of some small tools such as a seeddrill, a wheelhoe, shovels and forks. The remaining $200 would be set aside for living expenses - $10 a month for twenty months. In effect, the latter would be a continuation of the relief.

The $500 cost of the land, including the house lot, would be paid in easy installments in the following years when the settlers would be realizing some income from their labours.

Snor spread word of his plan around the immigrant communities in Ontario. That's when Van Dyke's ears perked up. Others, too, became interested. They saw a chance to press onward to better things. Moreover, having come from a country where 'polders' - reclaimed areas - were part of the landscape, the idea of moving to a diked-in area was alluring. The name, too, conjured up a feeling that they would soon be living in a small piece of Holland, which tended to instill a degree of comfort and reassurance.

Snor signed up seventeen Dutch immigrants: William Valenteyn, Jan Rupke, John van Dyke, Gerrit Brouwer, Abraham Havinga, Harm Prins, A. Barselaar, Marinus van Dyken, Ties Oosterhuis, Albert Biemold, Eeltje de Jong, Louis Boonstra, Jack van Luyk, Karsjen Miedema, Simon Winter, Henry Nienhuis and Jacob van der Goot. In addition, two non-Dutch people were recruited: Turner, an Englishman, and Meisner, a German.

Rupke, a friend of Snor, had been an enthusiastic supporter and promoter of the scheme while it was being discussed and developed. He wanted to be part of it. Although he was not capable of the hard physical work which settlement in the Marsh would require - the result of a bout with polio - he had a number of sons with strong arms and ambition.

Nearly all of the Dutch families lived in the Hamilton-Burlington area, and most of these belonged to the Christian Reformed Church there. Naturally, not everyone in the congregation was overjoyed by the news that many members would be leaving for the Marsh. This exodus would slice their number in half.

Nevertheless, the settlement program was a fait accompli. When all the arrangements were in place, most of the men who had signed up, and some of their older sons, travelled to the Marsh to make a start on developing their land and on building their houses.

That was in June, 1934.

Like most of the immigrants from the Netherlands, Snor retained a soft spot in his heart for anything Dutch, especially the food. Still, he regarded himself as a Canadian first, and he wanted other newcomers to harbour similar feelings.

And one way to get people to become part of the country was to spread them out instead of moving them to clusters, as was being done in some places.

So the settlement scheme, involving the establishment of a largely Dutch community, went totally counter to Snor's principles.

"He was bothered by that to some degree," said daughter Helen Sutton. "But there was no choice then, considering the economic climate. He figured that immigrants would always be employed if they were self-sustaining, no matter how difficult the times. If they worked for someone else, they could sudden-

George Postema checks over a field littered with tree roots.

The Ladies Aid from Hamilton is enjoying a picnic in 1931.
A few years later, many of these women were residents of the Marsh.

ly find themselves without a job. So if he could place them on a plot of land - their own plot - they at least would have a chance to be something in their new land."

Other Dutch people continued to check out the Marsh. A few decided to purchase some of the raw land independently and seed a crop of vegetables, holding in abeyance any plans to settle there. Among them was George C. Postema.

Word about the reclaimed area reached Postema, a native of Delft, near The Hague, in March, 1934. Life had not been easy since his emigration to Canada in 1928 at the age of twenty-four. He now thought: "Would this be an opportunity to get out of the shadow of the Depression?" He resolved to find out.

Early in May, he left Hamilton, accompanied by a number of friends: Roubos, who ran a flower nursery and greenhouse in nearby Stoney Creek; Van Ark, one of the founders of the Dutch settlement of Neerlandia in the western province of Alberta, and his son, William Jr. They drove at thirty-five miles an hour, the maximum allowable speed. The highways then had only two lanes, with no dividing line.

"The last part leading to the Marsh was just a dirt road, and not very good at that," recalled Postema. "To anyone having seen a flat expanse of prairie land, the Marsh from that point would have looked familiar, with no trees, no buildings and rimmed at the far distance by some greenery. It was plain that the whole area had been ploughed up, the wide furrows lying bare, with dead tree stumps everywhere sticking out of the ground. One could smell the soil - a peculiar smell not unlike that of the peat areas in the Peel district of Holland."

A small, lone shack stood at the entrance to the Marsh.

"We went in and a man, who introduced himself as a Mr. Snor, enquired immediately if each party wanted ten, twenty or more acres. After reminding him that this was not a dime department store, we started scrutinizing the mapped layout on the table, judging such things as accessibility to roads. Prices differed slightly. I joined up with Roubos on a ten-acre lot, with each responsible for five acres, while the Van Arks selected a larger area. Our land was priced at $190 an acre."

The next day, Postema and Roubos went to the owner of the land, who ran a large store in Hamilton, and signed the pa-

pers. Much planning on what to grow followed. There were even a few trips to the agricultural college at Guelph for helpful information and advice. Then the work started.

Commuting from the Hamilton area, the men spent all their free time preparing the land, seeding and planting, hoeing, pulling weeds and gathering up dead wood. They slept in a tent whenever they planned to make an early start in the field on the following day.

A dozen or so of the men who had moved to the Marsh to work on the settlement had a more solid roof over their heads - a henhouse section, twenty feet by twenty feet. It was the property of one of the settlers, Jan Rupke, who had tried his hand, unsuccessfully, at a chicken business at Ancaster, near Hamilton.

Rupke, the father of nine children - two had stayed behind in Holland - had moved the coop to the Marsh, opening it up for communal use.

"It served as a sitting room, living room, bedroom, meeting place and community centre all in one," explained John van

A village rises in the Marsh:
Abraham Havinga and John Rupke discuss its progress.

Dyke, who was there. "One can readily understand that many of the most necessary conveniences of life were totally missing. Night and day, very crowded conditions existed. There were a couple of double beds for the older men, but the younger fellows had to find a spot on the floor somehow. Orange crates served as chairs and as a storage place for each man's plates, forks, spoons and other personal belongings. Household duties were divided as fairly as possible; some were appointed hewers of wood and other were drawers of water. The water had to be carried by pail from a well a quarter of a mile away."

But then, some of the men were used to walking long distances. All the settlers had drawn lots to determine who would get what parcel. Valenteyn was the lucky one to get the field immediately behind the land set aside for the houses. Pity the ones who had to walk all the way towards the end of the tract whenever they wanted to get to their land.

~~~

Birth of a Village

The men of the henhouse were early risers. They barely had time for breakfast before hurrying outdoors. A lot of work needed to be done, and everyone wanted to make use of every minute of daylight.

"All our land had to be broken up," said John Van Dyke. "A man on a tractor ploughed and we walked behind him, pulling out numerous stumps and roots. There must have been a forest on that land at one time. Boy, there was a lot of wood that had to be cleared away."

Day in and day out, the men laboured in their fields, using little garden tools to even out the soil and get it ready for planting. Drainage ditches were dug by hand. Little wonder that the sweaty bodies were caked with dust and muck at the end of the long day.

The men took their baths in the nearby canal. Each had his own spot, screened by low-hanging branches at water's edge. They stripped naked and scrubbed themselves clean. The cool water seemed to ease the fatigue, and it wasn't unusual for someone to spontaneously bellow forth a refrain or two from his favourite Dutch ditty.

One day, this privacy was unexpectedly interrupted.

"A few of us were busy scrubbing the muck off our bodies," chuckled Van Dyke, "when a car came down the hill and stopped on the bridge a hundred feet away. A man and woman got out to enjoy the sights and the beauty of the setting sun. For us, the chance of being discovered was very real, despite the gathering dusk, so we all kept as quiet as a mouse. We didn't make one ripple on that water until the nature-loving couple went away, much to our relief. I'm sure that they would have seen nature from another angle had they discovered us."

The men, refreshed, headed for their one-room coop, where the cook, Jan Rupke, had prepared his standard meal of potatoes with lettuce, topped with a generous shot of sizzling suet. For the food, and the roof over their heads, the men were charged $1.50 a week, a cost they considered reasonable.

On most evenings, after the sun had gone down, the men sat around idly, discussing the progress being made in the fields and their theories on the type of crops that could be grown. And, of course, they chatted about the building of their little dwellings, a task which some had judged the most important. In fact, they often broke away from their slugging in the dirt to wield hammer and saw and move their places a step closer to partial completion. They were anxious to have their wives and children join them in their new surroundings.

The lumber was brought to the site by a truck. This was quite an undertaking, as there was no hard road - only a road allowance - leading into the Marsh at that point. The loads included eleven eight-foot cedar poles for each house, which enabled the men to build their dwellings three feet above ground level. This was a precautionary measure in case of a break in the dike and possible flooding. The word was out that this barrier was not sturdily built, consisting only of soil that came out of the canal.

The men were more familiar with agriculture than with carpentry. But they got lots of help and sound advice from Tony Sneep, the builder of the henhouse and a craftsman of sorts, who had been recruited as the superintendent of the building program.

"Tony showed us what to do," recalled Van Dyke. "He'd assemble a piece, let's say of the rafters, and we all had to do the same. This made it easier for us, speeded things up and cut down on the chances for mistakes."

He also looked after jobs that required the hand of an expert, such as the installation of doors and windows. For all his

Miles of drainage ditches were dug by hand.

*This is a view of the henhouse in which a dozen or so men lived.
After the houses were built, it remained on the site and was used for storage.*

plained Van Dyke. "Everyone pitched in. We grew all kinds of vegetables, which were divided evenly among us and kept us and our families fed during the harsh winter which lay ahead."

The men of the henhouse weren't spoiled by a good roast of beef or a juicy steak. And so everyone shouted with glee when one of the gang brought home a fat, furry animal he had cornered and unceremoniously killed.

"They called it a groundhog," said Van Dyke. "And because of the hog part in the name, we decided that this creature must be a distant member of the pig family and therefore should make a delicious meal."

Rupke sharpened his knife and promptly set to the task of cleaning the animal and roasting it in a big pan.

efforts, he charged $25 a house. When all was done, and he called on the owners for payment, he invariably collected only a few dimes, or a few quarters at the most. Such was the scarcity of available funds. One can imagine the number of visits that were required before the books were finally balanced.

The houses, simple in design, were built in a long row on the west side of the road allowance. The front windows looked out over an expanse of marshland, a section of the dike and beyond that some scenic wooded hills.

Rupke's dwelling, at the far end of the row, stood out from the rest; it had a more imaginative form. Son John explained: "We had some family in the States who knew a bit about construction. When they came over for a visit, they showed us how to build something with a bit of style for the same price." Sneep did most of the carpentry work on this house.

The houses consisted of a living room and a kitchen downstairs and two bedrooms on top. An outhouse, built a ways from the dwelling to prevent undesirable odours from drifting inside, would serve the family in hot weather and cold.

The only clean water for drinking, cooking, cleaning and bathing would have to be hauled by pail from a communal artesian well which tapped a generous stream 260 feet down. In time, contributions from friends in Holland would enable the settlers to buy sufficient pipe for carrying the water along the row of houses so that each family would have a supply of running water at their door.

Individual water lines would not be installed until 1943. Electricity would come sooner - in 1939.

Compared to the Canadian standards of the day, the lots were quite narrow - fifty feet - but the depth, at more than three times this amount, made up for that. There was lots of space for backyard gardens, where such favourites as *boerenkool* (kale) and endive could be grown. But with lots of other work receiving priority in the first year, the working of the little plots was put on the back burner.

"That first year, we had a community garden of three acres as no one really had time to look after a garden of his own," ex-

Tony Sneep works on one of the houses.

The Dutch settlement is rising quickly.

When the fields were ready, or reasonably so, an attempt was made at growing a few crops. It was more of an experiment, to see what would grow besides weeds. The settlers, at that time, seemed more concerned about the success of their common garden, making sure there would be a good supply of such staples as potatoes, onions and carrots, and about getting their houses ready for occupancy.

In the fall of 1934, some of the dwellings were completed to the point where people could move in. In reality, however, they were nothing more than a shell.

But the wives and their children just couldn't wait any longer, and they moved to the Marsh at the earliest possible opportunity.

When they descended the hill to the valley for the first time, and their eyes took in the desolate terrain, doubts surfaced, albeit fleetingly, about the wisdom of moving to such an isolated, undeveloped area, with all the uncertainties. This feel-

Jan Rupke's house stood out from the others.

"With fitting ceremony, the pan was put on the table and the lid was lifted off. There lay this delicious morsel. The cook had taken the hide off all right, but the legs were still on. The sight of four paws with sharp claws sticking upward robbed most of us of an appetite. The cook, however, was brave enough to go at it with knife and fork and nibbled away. Marinus van Dyken also took a bite or two. But they quickly gave up, and the whole thing was thrown out."

On another occasion, a pair of new arrivals innocently brought a skunk to the henhouse. This time, the animal didn't get past Rupke. But the coop had to be aired out and the clothes of the duo had to hang on the outside line for three weeks before everything could be declared odour-free.

There weren't too many neighbours around in those early days. In fact, the only ones in the immediate area of the settlement were two single men of Italian origin who lived in a shack and grew celery. With no irrigation, their crop did not amount to much, and they disappeared soon after the arrival of the Dutch colonists. A number of people lived along the northern fringe of the Marsh, near the Bradford Marsh, but, with no ready access to that area from the interior, they seemed so far away.

A few growers who had bought land without government assistance were often spotted working in the muck. But they did not live in the Marsh - not yet. Only after the settlement had sprung up did shacks, garages and other structures make a gradual appearance.

An artesian well provided plenty of fresh water.

ing was experienced even by those who arrived later.

Elsey Havinga, who later married Cor Sneep, surveyed the bleak landscape from atop a load of furniture on a stake truck and immediately thought: "So this is what is meant by the statement 'God-forsaken country'."

But such sentiments were quickly overtaken by the excitement, the anticipation, the realization that this was a place that truly could be called home.

A skunk emits an obnoxious odour when frightened.

The groundhog is not edible.

~~~

Beyond the Winter

Winter came early for the families who had moved into their new homes on the Marsh. The snow was deep and the little colony was frequently isolated. At times, some of the men struggled on foot through waist-deep drifts to reach Bradford for supplies. They once made their way through a blinding blizzard, linked to each other with a rope.

"That winter was a particularly cold one," recalled John van Dyke. "The houses were not finished off inside and they were very hard to heat. The only fuel we had were the roots and stumps cleared from the fields. These were fed into our stoves constantly."

Some families nailed empty fertilizer bags over the studs inside and then hid these with wallpaper. Others did likewise with cardboard boxes. This did lessen the drafts from the cold winds howling pitilessly across the open terrain. But it didn't warm up the rooms.

"My stove was red hot all day just to keep the downstairs warm," said Van Dyke. "Fortunately, our supply of wood was plentiful, and we didn't have to scrounge for that. I was the first one up in the morning; the others had to stay in bed. I put on my overcoat, my mitts and my shoes and tried to get warm while I got the stove started. I could see ice on the ceiling. After forty-five minutes, the room was sufficiently heated to enable me to call the family."

John Rupke recalls going downstairs and seeing ice on the pail of water behind the stove, which doubled as the cooking appliance. As he was lying in bed, snuggled under a pair of blankets, he had spotted frost on the nails sticking out of the ceiling, so the ice in the bucket did not come as a total surprise. Still, the sight of it was unsettling.

When the wind blew hard, which it often did, the houses swayed. That's because they were sitting on poles.

"This gave us an eerie, insecure feeling," said Van Dyke. "But our concerns were lessened somewhat whenever we reminded ourselves that these shells were our very own homes, and that if we stuck it out and earned some money, we could eventually improve them to a comfortable state. Looking back, it all seems so primitive. And I suppose it was. But we didn't notice it so much at the time. After all, all of us were in the same boat. I must emphasize the unity among the group. We realized that we had to stick together through thick and thin. No one felt superior. We all didn't have a cent to our names. Our only way to go was up, through hard work and dedication. And we did stick it out."

Later, the houses were raised and concrete basements were poured. And annexes were added on to some, eliminating the need for two or three children to sleep in one bed and for curtains to separate the sleeping quarters of the boys and girls.

George Postema, who owned land outside the settlement, spent the winter in Hamilton, agonizing over his future. Should he return in the spring to seed another crop? Or should he get out and head for other endeavours?

Doubts about continuing for another season had already arisen in the fall of 1934 when the produce taken off the new land had to be marketed. The customers weren't exactly lining up. Few people had heard of the Marsh and its products.

The carrots and potatoes were holed-in in long rows, then covered with earth as protection against the early frosts which were known to strike low-lying areas. When everything was out

The Dutch settlement with its distinctive look.

The men take a break from their community chores.

of the ground, it was trucked to the greenhouse in Stoney Creek of colleague Roubos. Perhaps it could be sold in the cities.

"But with the oncoming winter," said Postema, "much had to be left behind. And it proved to be a slow process selling the produce to stores, restaurants and hotels. Buyers were choosy. And in midwinter, the government even required regrading of the potatoes, which made it all but impossible to get rid of the stored-up crop. As a matter of fact, it could not even be given away."

As he pondered the time to come, Postema thought of all the expenses he had incurred, including the land purchase, the many hours spent on preparing the fields and growing and harvesting, and all the headaches involved in transporting truckload after truckload of unsold vegetables and storing this all.

"We decided to sell the now much-improved marshland, cleared and worked, back to the original owners at just the purchase price."

Moving on to other things, Postema successfully passed the exams for radio telegraphist. During the Second World War, which started in 1939, he was employed by the federal government for intercepting code signals to and from German naval stations, with particular atten-

Jacob van der Goot, complete with wooden shoes, gets ready to start another working day.

tion focused on the U-boats. Until his retirement, he stuck with the government's telecommunications department, specializing in radio frequencies - certainly a far cry from groping around in the black muck.

The people of the settlement never entertained thoughts of leaving - at least not openly. The bleak winter ended and spring came. It was time to sow another crop.

There was another important affair: the naming of the colony. Some of the senior men, including Jan Rupke, agreed on Ansnorveldt [1]). It's a combination of the Dutch words 'aan' and 'veld' and the name Snor, meaning On Snor's Field.

"Mr. Rupke came to me - I was a teen then - and asked: 'Do you think your Dad would object if we named this place after him?'" recalled Helen Sutton, Snor's daughter. "I told him he would consider it an honour."

A flagpole was raised at the north end of the settlement. All the residents were summoned to the spot, and they gathered in a circle. First the Canadian ensign was raised, followed by the Dutch flag. Rupke then spoke a few words, extending appreciation to Snor for all he had done to make the settlement a reality.

The name was now official.

[1]) Commonly spelled Ansnorveld.

The men and their sons get together to check out and discuss the progress of the crops.

In a way, all immigrants are pioneers. They say goodbye to much of what is dear and familiar and strike out resolutely for alien shores, intending to delve into the unknown and emerge somehow in a better world.

The cluster of Marsh people, however, had gone a step further: while still adjusting themselves to a different culture, language, climate and geography, they had decided to move to an area where, figuratively, no one had been before and launch a new existence from scratch.

People so bold must possess certain qualities: an imagination to see a future few others can perceive, perseverance to pull them through unthinkable situations, a willingness to get by with only the bare necessities, an ingenuity to work wonders with next to nothing, lots of optimism, and faith in themselves and in God.

The settlers of Ansnorveldt came out of that severe first winter intact, anxious to get on with the business of making a living. True, the pioneering virtues had been put to the test when they had been surrounded for weeks on end by a white wilderness. But

The famous henhouse stood behind Jan Rupke's dwelling.

now that the snow had melted, and the black soil had reappeared, everyone was anxious as ever to get at the land.

The men, some with wooden shoes, waded through mud to get to their fields. They were hardly recognizable when they returned for lunch or supper. The women, who had spent a big part of their day cleaning up inside and out, saw no end to their task. But there were few complaints.

When the muck dried a bit under the warm sun, and such tasks as fertilizing and seeding were possible, the women and the older children also went to the fields to help out. And there was no shortage of work later on in the season: thinning plants, weeding, harvesting, or merely pulling out tree roots which still seemed to be everywhere.

While they groped around in the muck, some of the women also had to keep an eye on their toddlers. For them, there was no such thing as idleness. When father called it a day in the fields, mother still had hours of work ahead of her at home.

In the ensuing years, after many difficulties had been conquered and the Marsh was generally regarded as an agrarian success, the men who were frequently thrust into the limelight would quickly

The entrance sign to the Dutch settlement.

point to their spouses and say: "None of this would have happened to the extent it did without their hard work, at home and in the fields, and their support and encouragement when times were tough."

Many of the growers today volunteer similar sentiments. One remarked: "The role of the women is underplayed. You always hear about the men. But behind every successful man stands a woman, and this is especially true in the Marsh. The wives were always ready to pitch in, during the day or in the evening. They were the best labourers the farmers had. Without their help, the Marsh would have been quite a different place."

In the early years, the daily routine for the adults and the older children consisted of work, work, work, which left little time for relaxation or other pursuits.

This little store was an extension to one of the houses in Ansnorveldt. It changed ownership a number of times before going out of business.

"Those were hard times, that's for sure," commented John Van Dyke. "But a tremendous community spirit existed among the pioneers. We did everything together and we divided love and sorrow. Together we experimented because, yes, in the beginning we really didn't know the soil - what it could do, what it needed - and what crops would grow best. It took a few years for us to get some experience under our belts."

Potatoes, carrots and lettuce were grown in good quantity. Some of the settlers also tried celery, but were disappointed in the result. With proper management of the soil still a ways off, the land simply was too dry during the heat of summer.

To the naked eye, the black muck at Ansnorveldt looked extremely rich and capable of supporting any crop. That's why, at first, it was highly prized. Later on, it was realized that the lighter peat land in the centre of the Marsh was far more productive.

Experience determined that a great deal of chemical fertilizer had to be applied to the soil in the spring to supply a long list of lacking nutrients. Actually, all the muck did was support the roots and hold moisture for the plant - it provided little or no nourishment.

And then there were the dust storms, especially during dry periods. The wind lifted the arid soil and sent it through the air in a suffocating cloud. It drifted like snow, banking up around buildings and filling in the drainage ditches. Even today, it's a constant battle to keep the precious stuff from blowing away.

Some of the newcomers didn't hesitate to walk over the land to Bradford and ask Professor Day, an acknowledged expert, for advice on how to overcome certain problems. He gave this freely. In fact, he marvelled at the enthusiasm of the pioneers and their inherent belief in the future of the Marsh - his Marsh.

Other immigrants from Hamilton, and even Chatham, stopped by for a look. They readily volunteered their advice and opinions, even though they generally lacked experience in muck farming. The real reason behind their visits was always obvious: they just wanted to engage in small talk to find out what Holland Marsh was all about.

Not long after the arrival of the Dutch settlers, an insurance company in Bradford, Nolan and Green, promoted an interesting scheme for building a gardening community on two hundred acres of land it owned a short distance north of Ansnorveldt. The principals of this firm obviously were impressed with what John Snor had been able to accomplish, and they had visions of attracting more people to the Marsh as permanent residents by making housing sites and allotments readily available.

Snor himself wholeheartedly endorsed the subdivision plan in published comments in June, 1935: "To be able to purchase a five-acre unit ready for seeding, with a four-room house and garden located in the community centre, including running water and all privileges connected with the community, for as low as $1,000, should interest a large number of gardeners, including a number of our Hollanders, and I for one will recommend it to our people."

He actually urged Bradford officials to give attention to the building of a direct road to the Marsh - "otherwise I am afraid a new town will be in the making before long, within two miles of us, with its own stores and places of business."

Alas, despite all the enthusiasm, the subdivision never came to fruition. In the midst of the Depression, not enough interest could be generated among prospective growers to warrant the scheme to proceed. Money and confidence were decidedly lacking.

The land, still unbroken, was then offered for sale at the bargain price of $40 an acre. It was grabbed up quickly, despite the scarcity of cash.

"You know, a couple hundred dollars would give you five acres of it," said Van Dyke. "It would have to be broken up and brought into shape for production. But after that, the value jumped considerably. It turned out to be a good investment for those who were able to scrape the money together."

While much of the focus seemed to be on the land, life in the village did not stand still. A clay road had been put in front of the row of houses, improving access. One of the regular visitors to the place was a storekeeper in Bradford.

"We bought milk and groceries, which he carried in his little wagon," recalled Van Dyke. "He knew we didn't have a nickel to spare and gladly extended us credit. He told us: 'If you haven't got the money, don't worry. I'll put it on the bill. Pay me in the fall after the crops are sold.' He had good faith in the Dutch people. We paid him when we had a few cents left over."

Later, Henry Nienhuis, one of the settlers, seeing an opportunity for extra income, opened a little store in his home and put his wife in charge. Once a week, she went all the way to Richmond Hill, near Toronto, to pick up her wholesale stock; the suppliers didn't think it was worth their while to come to the Marsh. The store expanded into an addition to the house.

When the hot weather arrived, and preserving the precious food became a concern, some of the men crawled under their houses and dug deep holes. Milk and other perishable provisions were thus stored underground and kept reasonably cool.

Cars were scarce in Ansnorveldt. And public transportation was non-existent. Van Dyke, for one, often felt isolated, cut off from the rest of the world.

"My wife was in the Toronto General Hospital for eight weeks for observation and tests. I made a point of visiting her twice a week. But the only way I could get to Toronto was by hitch-hiking. I left early in the morning so that I could be at the hospital by one o'clock. I often wouldn't be home again until ten o'clock at night."

While he was away, a few of the women of the settlement would look after his three boys, aged two, four and six.

"Conditions were doubly hard for me at that time. Mother was in the hospital and I had to look after three young boys and the crop of vegetables too. But we had so much help from the ladies in various ways."

Owning a car was one of the goals of most of the settlers. But that would take money. As a rule, the banks extended credit only to those people who could repay promptly and regularly. As agriculture in the Marsh was largely unproven and, in some eyes, unpromising, the ones without cars had no alternative but to wait until they had saved up enough cash.

Above:
Simon Visser
converted an old
truck into a tractor.
It did its job, and
stood as a good
example of
ingenuity employed
during difficult
times.

Here's another
makeshift tractor,
the proud
possession of John
van Dyke.

Simon Visser, who had independently purchased ten acres of land north of the settlement, provided an invaluable and popular service in the early years: his truck, the only one in the immediate area, often doubled as a bus.

"It could hold about ten people," he recalled. "They would sit on benches. A canvas kept out the elements. If a group of people wanted to go on an outing to Toronto or to some other place, I'd charge them a few dimes for the ride to cover my expenses."

He had bought the truck in 1932 when he started up a business in the Hamilton area, selling and delivering fruit and vegetables in summer and coal and wood in winter. He also moved furniture, regardless of the season. But for all his endeavours, he made little money.

After moving to the Marsh, Visser built a double garage on his land, reserving the first half for his truck and the other half for himself. He slept on a mattress placed on the dirt floor. But he didn't mind. It was still an improvement over his first days in Canada, in the Sarnia area of Ontario in 1928, when the farmer he worked for told him and Mrs. Visser to bring in straw from the barn so that they would have something to sleep on. Visser later extended his garage, and even built a storey on top, so that his wife, who had stayed behind in Hamilton, could rejoin him in comfortable living quarters.

Another priority for him was to get acquainted with the distinctive soil. He really had no experience with vegetable growing. In fact, when he lived in Holland, he had operated his own cargo boat from Akkrum to Leeuwarden and Sneek. Now he was a landlubber, frequently seeking the advice of other settlers.

But with the truck he was king. He gladly would drive people to church in Hamilton or to the Canadian National Exhibition in Toronto. He also delivered the produce of others to the markets in Bradford, Toronto and elsewhere.

"We couldn't do without that truck," said one old-timer, with a twinge of nostalgia. "And neither could the storekeepers in Bradford. They got together and paid Visser to take people from the Marsh on shopping trips to the town. They wanted the business, of course."

The onion harvest is being processed in the field.

This was Simon Visser's business card. Note the anglicized spelling of his name, not a rare practice among early immigrants. He never did legally change it though.

~~~

Spooky Things

Fifteen-year-old Wilma van der Goot didn't bother completing the few weeks left of her high school term after her family moved to their house in Ansnorveldt in May, 1935.

"I registered at the high school in Bradford and found the subjects were different from those I had taken in Burlington," explained Wilma, who married Stoffer Oosterhuis, a son of one of the original settlers, in 1942. "So I didn't go. Besides, I had to help my father in the fields."

Jacob van der Goot's allotment was the farthest away, requiring a ten-minute walk. Wilma didn't even have a bicycle to make travel quicker. That was a luxury the family could ill afford.

But all that walking came in good stead for later. When the new school year started in September, Wilma enrolled in grade 10 and walked to Bradford each day, rain or shine. Usually accompanied by another Dutch girl, she left the house at 7:15 and arrived at school by 8:30.

"In the winter, when it was often bitterly cold, this half hour before the start of classes gave us a chance to thaw out," she recalled. "Girls didn't wear slacks then; it was unheard of for girls to go to school without dresses. That's all changed now. And there are school buses too."

The girls also ran errands. Residents along their walking route quite often asked them to pick up certain goods at stores in Bradford. They happily obliged, knowing there was a good possibility they would get a ride back to Ansnorveldt in a delivery vehicle.

Wilma later got an after-school job as a live-in babysitter in Bradford. This meant that the long walks had virtually come to an end. She got free room and board in lieu of pay. On Saturday afternoons, with no further need for her services, she walked home to spend the weekend with her family.

This arrangement ended in March, 1937, when her mother, Eelkje, died of a chronic kidney disease at the age of forty-five. It was the first death in the tiny community, and everyone was grieved. Wilma now had to leave school to assume the household chores and look after her little brother, Ted, while Dad worked in the fields.

Ted, born in Burlington, where his parents had located after moving from Makkum, in Friesland, in 1929, had also

One of the critters hauled out of the canal.

marked a first. On June 6, 1935, he had become the first baby to be baptized in the settlement. This event had taken place in the home of his parents, a short time before the growing church group would cease using individual homes for services and move into a little building of their own.

Dense bush once covered large areas of the valley. Some of this was taken off during the lumbering operations. More of it was cleared when the land was about to be opened up, enhancing the prospects of attracting investors and growers. Still, a lot of trees remained in a few areas in the latter half of the 1930's.

A path led through the woods to a few cabins along the fringe of the southwestern section. Someone in the settlement once commented with genuine concern: "I wouldn't go there alone at night. I'd never come out alive."

Indeed, some of the settlers, perhaps influenced by stories they had read in Holland about bears, wolves and Indian savages roaming the Canadian wilds, feared to venture outdoors after the sun had gone down. Such concerns, of course, were far-fetched. Although nocturnal critters did abound, none was of the ferocious type, and the stereotyped image of native people was certainly erroneous.

Some years later, Simon Winter, one of the pioneers, said in a speech laced with historical tidbits: "The improvised roads - mere mud puddles - were bordered by age-old stumps, towering spruce and cedar trees, poplars which always seemed to rustle, and an assortment of undergrowth. And although we weren't in Africa, where lions sometimes appeared from such groves, we did have creatures to contend with. There were four-legged ones with a bad habit of pulling out our carrots while everyone was soundly asleep."

The settlers also had to put up with swarms of mosquitoes, prolific breeders in the marshy areas. These insects made it impossible for the few men with guns to remain motionless while lying in wait in the darkness to catch the carrot snatchers in the act. The element of surprise was spoiled and the thieves, whatever species they may have been, got a reprieve.

Simon Winter

In his talk, Winter also recalled the abundance of large fish - probably carp - in the river and the canal. "If you went to the river at four o'clock in the afternoon, you could already hear them splashing and playing from a distance of five hundred feet." Regrettably, their numbers have declined in great measure over the years.

Not only carrot thieves found a haven in the woods; the dense growth in areas east of the Marsh provided ideal cover for an illegal whisky-making operation.

"It was an open secret," said Mrs. Wilma Oosterhuis, "that some people at Holland Landing, woodcutters by trade, ran whisky stills in the bush. That was in the days of prohibition, when bootlegging wasn't that uncommon. My father had run across one such operation on Walpole Island, beyond Chatham, where he had gone to look for a job in the pre-Marsh days. And here we had one right on our doorstep."

The bush was a ready source of firewood whenever the piles of roots and stumps gathered from the fields dwindled in size. No one had money to spare for coal. In the spring, when the growers ploughed their land, more roots would be exposed. As before, they would be gathered, placed in piles for drying and then be used in the kitchen stove for cooking and heating.

"Even today, after all these years, we still come across the odd root," said a grower with land near Ansnorveldt.

Later, when the heating systems were improved and the

Eelkje van der Goot and her son Ted.

Eise Biemold uses a tractor-powered saw to cut up piles of tree roots and stumps removed from his land.

John van Dyke dusts his crops during the 1937 season.

roots were no longer needed, some of the piles were set on fire. This practice was frowned on, however. Fires in organic soil can spread rapidly underground and are extremely difficult to check.

"The wood for our fences also came from the bush," explained Mrs. Oosterhuis. "Some of these fences were really fancy. Families tried to outdo each other. The end result was fine, as the appearance of the settlement really improved."

In 1936, Ansnorveldt lost two residents: Gerrit Brouwer and his wife decided to move back to Holland. She had suffered from severe bouts of homesickness.

That news created many long faces. The solidarity of which everyone had been so proud, and which had helped everyone so tremendously, had crumbled a bit. But this setback was quickly forgotten when another Dutch family moved in - that of Jan Rupke's brother, Johan, who had originally emigrated to New Jersey in the U.S.

The news of the departure of the Brouwer couple paled in comparison with the shocking word that spread like wildfire across the Marsh early on July 1 that year.

"A frost hit on the last day of June, totally ruining our potato crop," recalled John van Dyke. "When we got up in the morning, the plants were black. The entire village, young and old, walked around in a daze. There was a feeling of despair. People asked themselves and each other: 'Wouldn't it be better to give up? We can't continue to live here if there's frost in the middle of summer.' But then one of the older residents came forward and said: 'Listen, God brought us here and He had a purpose in doing so. We can't give up.' Ashamed, we admitted that he was right. And we continued on."

Between the potato beds, the growers planted carrots, lettuce and cabbage.

"And you know what? We still had a good year. After that terrible frost, it became abnormally hot, and everywhere else the crops withered. But not in the Marsh. The ground here holds moisture and the temperature is always a few degrees lower. We were the only ones with a good harvest - a harvest we had no trouble marketing."

Any group of people engaged in a substantial endeavour requires a leader. In Ansnorveldt, Jan Rupke emerged as one. When there was a problem, people went to him to get it straightened out.

He became generally known as the 'burgemeester', a word even the Canadians got to understand after awhile.

"It already started in the henhouse," explained Van Dyke. "All matters of interest to the group were discussed and settled - or not settled - there. Such meetings were also held in his house

Some of the settlers pose for a group photo.

Mr. and Mrs. Jan Rupke and four of their children prior to emigration.

later on. Problems - and they were plentiful - were tackled under his leadership. In the first years, it wasn't easy sailing for any of us, so a good leader was badly needed. And Rupke, with the help of other older men like Abraham Havinga and Albert Biemold, fit the bill."

Rupke, who came to Canada in 1929 from Oud-Loosdrecht, north of Utrecht, did have more time on his hands than the other settlers. His physical handicap prevented him from doing most manual work. This he left in the hands of his children. But he still ran the show.

His son John, fourteen at the time of emigration, recalled: "He was adamant in getting the right price for our celery so as to cover all the costs and make a bit of profit too. He'd figure it all out on a piece of paper. If he couldn't get his price for a crate, he'd refuse to sell it. He wanted to keep it in storage, hoping to sell it when the price was higher. But this seldom worked in those days. We often had to dump the celery."

Still, people gave him high marks for trying. They knew that he had the welfare of all growers at heart.

Woodcutters are at work, clearing more land.

After the development of Ansnorveldt, efforts were continued to attract more settlers to the Marsh. More land is prepared for seeding and planting. Before long, there are bountiful crops.

"People from Bradford who visited the Marsh and saw the Rupke house, which stood out from the others, assumed that the mayor lived there," said one settler. "We didn't want to tell them we didn't have a mayor, because we wouldn't have told the whole truth."

If Rupke could be called a father of the Marsh, so could John Snor, who got the Dutch people there in the first place. He and his wife, living in a beautiful house in Bradford, retained an active interest in the well-being of everyone. They often stopped by for a chat to find out how things were going.

"We're getting by," was the typical comment. "Just barely though."

Snor found most of the people at peace with themselves, as if they had grown accustomed to their hardships. They seemed to realize that they had been handed a golden opportunity to use their hands and heads and make something of their lives in a time when countless others were still out of work and subsisting merely by the kind graces of the government. Few other alternatives had been open to them.

"Before we moved here," said Mrs. Oosterhuis, "Dad was out of work and we were on welfare. When he heard about Holland Marsh, and that the government would help financially, he applied right away. He figured that anything was better than being on relief - it was a dirty word. I'm sure that's what kept most of them going during those harsh years."

For the people who had been on welfare, and for those who had not, moving to the Marsh did not bring about quick changes in their living standard, as we've already seen. It was tough slugging, especially for the large families. There never seemed to be enough money for household items and clothes.

This did not escape the eye of Snor's wife, Cornelia.

"She was a good seamstress," said Mrs. Oosterhuis, "and she organized an evening class and gave handicraft lessons to the teenaged girls, figuring that we could help with the clothing problem. The classes were held in the public school, which had been built in the settlement in 1935, and all the teens took part. The material was supplied. I made a tailored suit and two dresses. You can imagine how proud I was."

Snor sometimes got under the skin of a few residents, mainly because he exuded an overbearing attitude.

"He was not always popular," admitted his daughter, Helen Sutton. "He sometimes was ruthless. If he was going to do something, nothing could stand in his way. But he was a man you could love and hate at the same time. Deep within, he had a lot of kindness."

It was Snor who ordered milk to be sent to the Marsh when some people had no other way of getting it. And his car always was available for emergencies, such as transporting a sick person to hospital.

Most of the trees on the Marsh disappeared eventually, as more land was cleared and made ready for vegetable production. The distant sounds of woodcutters at work frequently broke the silence that hung over the fields.

Outside the Marsh, private enterprise and individual farmers would undertake their own drainage schemes, adding another four thousand acres of productive muck land. Areas on both

In his post-Marsh days, John Snor was popular among flower enthusiasts. They stopped in droves at the Holland Bulb Company in Port Credit to admire two acres of colourful blooms. Snor is shown being interviewed outside his office. Inset: Cornelia Snor.

sides of the river from Bradford to Cook's Bay would be reclaimed, bearing such names as Colbar Marsh and Keswick Marsh. Reclamation would also take place in the nearby Cookstown and Alliston districts.

The remaining muck areas, totalling two thousand acres, would be set aside by the Ontario Ministry of Natural Resources for wildlife preservation.

In time, the population of the eleven thousand acres of marshland under cultivation in the Bradford area would reach three and a half thousand.

The two non-Dutch families in Ansnorveldt, the Turners and the Meisners, were true pioneers like the others, with their own little houses and five-acre plots.

Van Dyke, who lived between them, remembered the following:

"Mr. Turner, who was English, was a veteran of the First World War. While fighting the Germans, he got a dose of mustard gas, which affected his health for the rest of his life. He could never be exposed to the sun. If he did, he would break out in an awful, painful rash. He was never seen working his land; his teenage kids did the field work. He and his family lived quite well; perhaps he had a veteran's pension. Anyway, they stayed in the Marsh for only four to five years before leaving for the city. Meisner, a German, also left after three or four years. He was a tailor by occupation. I guess both Turner and Meisner never felt at home among all those Dutch people."

Snor's display at the Canadian National Exhibition in Toronto won him a coveted Gold Medal Award.

~~~

Their Inner Strength

For the men who lived in the henhouse in the summer of 1934, Sunday was a welcome day of rest. With a background deeply rooted in Calvinism, they adhered to the instruction in their Bible: "Six days you shall labour and do all your work, but the seventh day is a Sabbath day to the Lord your God. On it you shall not do any work."

And so most of them went to their wives and children for the weekend and attended church services in their respective communities. But there weren't enough cars and pickup trucks around to transport everyone, so some had to stay in the Marsh to pass a quiet, and lonely, day.

On Sunday, July 15, four of the stranded - Abraham Havinga, Albert Biemold, Harm Prins and Jan Rupke - decided to hold a religious service in the coop. But it turned uncomfortably hot that morning, so the table was moved outdoors and placed in the dirt. Havinga read a sermon. There was even an attempt at singing a hymn.

However brief and informal, the service gave these devout men an invigorating feeling that left their spiritual needs satisfied.

From then on, devotions were held at the coop each Sunday until the first houses had been completed to the point where some of the families could move in. On September 15, a group of people, including some women and children, gathered in the Biemold home, the first one occupied. The following Sunday, everyone went to another house, and so on down the line.

"This arrangement was soon known as the travelling church," said John van Dyke. "Everyone was required to bring his or her own chair, so it was a common sight on Sunday morning to see father carrying a chair for himself and one for mother. Junior would take care of his own, balancing it on top of his head."

That winter, some fifty people crowded into one of the small homes twice each Sunday. The services were in the Dutch language; the men who were called on to read sermons hadn't mastered English yet beyond a few basic greetings. It was a real treat when Rev. John S. Balt, pastor of the Christian Reformed Church in Hamilton, the mother congregation, came over to conduct a service. A Sunday school also was started, with Mrs. Havinga as teacher.

"This was the beginning of a growing church," recalled Van Dyke. "More and more people from Hamilton, Chatham and Windsor moved into the vicinity. Quite a few single men too. In the spring of 1935, it became evident that the homes were too small to contain the crowds for Sunday worship. The floors began to sag from the weight and had to be jacked up again. Some people began to object to this - and with reason. Something had to be done."

A few seriously toyed with the idea of splitting the group in two and holding four services. But there was no wide support for this. Most were leaning toward the construction of a church building, even though they realized this would be an undertaking they could hardly afford.

Simon Winter, one of the pioneers, recalled in a speech in 1963 that people

The Biemold home, where residents gathered for worship.

Inset: Abraham Havinga

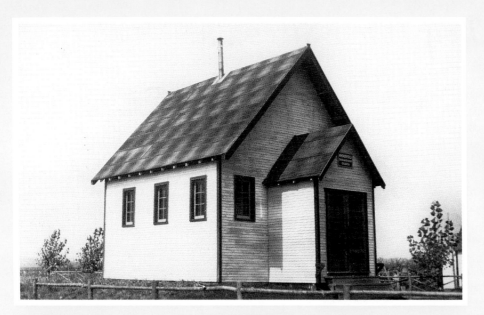

The finished church was a handsome addition to the fledgling community.

didn't have much money to spare: "In the early days, the collection once totalled thirty-eight cents. Later, things improved a bit and we got $3 to $4 for the church and around $2.50 for the deacon fund."

An enormous sum - $200 - was needed for building a small church, twenty feet by twenty feet, on an undeveloped lot at the southern end of the settlement. After three group meetings, it was decided to go ahead with the project.

"There was a cash balance of $75 on hand, which was a fine start," recounted Van Dyke. "And a trip to the bank was crowned with success. A loan of $175 was secured after it was backed by the signatures of a dozen or so men. I'm sure the signatures were all they had to back it with. So up went the little pioneer church."

Tony Sneep, who had already hammered many a nail in the settlement, was put in charge. He bought the lumber and other materials in Aurora, a nearby community, for $185. The men of the congregation kept the labour costs to a minimum, donating a total of 554 hours of work. There was a further saving when a Methodist church in Ancaster, near Hamilton, donated a pulpit and pews, all still in good shape.

June 21, 1935, was a happy day in the village. That's when the finished shell, built on cedar posts, out of the reach of water, was dedicated to the Lord's service. Rev. Balt travelled from Hamilton to officiate.

Mind you, not everyone in the Marsh was Reformed. That was true also in the village: one family was Roman Catholic, another went to a United Church and the two non-Dutch ones seldom attended church anywhere. Still, everyone could feel proud that another advancement had been made in the fledgling community.

"Finishing off the interior of the church had to wait until later, when there would be enough money for it," said Van Dyke. "However, this could not be postponed too long. The building was clad only with one layer of wood siding. The siding dried out and knotholes appeared.

This created somewhat of a problem: some of the younger set, and even some of the older ones, at times took more notice of the beauty of nature outside than of the man on the pulpit. Eventually, the little church was lined with wallboard and began to look more like a finished product - and much easier to heat during the cold winter ahead."

A big drum-like wood stove stood at the back of the church, nearly roasting the people sitting close to it in the winter. Conversely, the ones in the front pews braved a temperature not far from the freezing point. Later, after electricity had come to the Marsh, a wall fan was installed to effect a more uniform environment. Unfortunately, it did have an annoying tendency to compete with the voice from the pulpit.

Eise Biemold somehow got an old pump organ to produce melodious and inspiring accompaniment. The fact that he had his whole heart in the effort surely helped.

Above: Rev. John S. Balt   *This view of the rear of the settlement shows the church at the extreme right.*

Inset: Eise Biemold

He graduated from a little pump organ to an electronic instrument.

He had already become a serious student of the organ long before leaving Assen, in the province of Drenthe, in 1926 and sailing for Canada by himself at the age of seventeen. His father, Albert, who ran a wholesale bicycle business, would move the rest of the family to Canada shortly after. They all settled in the Chatham area, where they became acquainted with other Dutch immigrants at the young congregation of the Christian Reformed Church.

Of course, Eise played the organ there. One chronicler noted later: "Well qualified for the task, he never missed a service even though he lived with his parents some thirty miles from Chatham. For sheer faithfulness, few organists have such a record."

In 1928, tired of menial jobs on farms and in construction, Biemold headed west and landed at the sugarbeet farm of Bernard Nieboer at Iron Springs, Alberta. After a short stay, he moved back east and, together with the rest of his family, settled in Hamilton, where they scraped by with an assortment of jobs. The elder Biemold moved to the Marsh in 1934; Eise didn't get there until the following year.

"I enjoyed playing the organ in the little church," he recalled with a note of nostalgia. "I can remember the people sitting near that stove being burned to crisp. Maybe they preferred it to being frozen."

Tony Sneep and Nelly Rupke were married in the Ansorveldt church on October 17, 1937.

He had paid $50 down for ten acres of land. He grew potatoes and lettuce and some other commodities. But he just couldn't make a go of it. He went broke, unable to meet the payments, gave up and returned to Hamilton. There he started up a butter and egg route.

"But Dad was always anxious to have me back in Marsh. And I had a feeling for the work. So when he offered me a deal for ten acres, I sold my route and went back. That was in the spring of '42. I had married in the meantime. We built a double garage and lived in half of it. Orange crates stacked three or four high served as our cupboards. A year later, we added a kitchen. And gradually the garage became a house."

He continued to live in it until his death in the autumn of 1992.

The first wedding in the little church took place on a Sunday afternoon in mid-October, 1937, with most of the Dutch community looking on. Nelly Rupke exchanged vows with Tony Sneep, the carpenter, during the regular afternoon service conducted by Rev. Balt.

"It was a matter of economics," explained the daughter of Jan Rupke. "We counted our pennies in those days, and there was no choice but to keep everything simple and without frills. After the service, though, we had a little party at home, and friends and neighbours came over to offer congratulations. We provided tea, cake, cookies, fancy sandwiches - and even a glass of wine."

The next day, the groom reported to his new boss, a Dutch contractor in Brampton, just northwest of Toronto, who had hired him at the princely wage of fifty cents an hour. Later, he became a grower in the Marsh.

The marriage produced four children. But it came to an abrupt end in 1948 when Sneep suffered a fatal heart attack. His widow married Joe Brands, also a market gardener, one and a half years later.

As a result of the growing membership, the church was enlarged in 1938 by fifty feet, including eight feet for a meeting room for the consistory and a number of societies.

These groups bore Dutch names. The senior young people's one was called 'Wees een Zegen,' the junior group 'Het Mosterdzaadje' and the men's society 'Calvijn.' That's because

These young ladies are performing with the church choir.

Dutch lingered as the predominant language, particularly among the grownups. A journalist from Holland who passed through the settlement was startled, being so far away from home, to hear people freely singing such popular songs as 'Waar de Blanke Top der Duinen' and 'In 't Stille Dal, in 't Groene Dal.'

It was a different story with the younger ones, many of whom had been born in Canada. They became more conversant in English, through attendance at school and association with other youngsters. Inevitably, there was a gradual move away from the use of Dutch, even in the Sunday services. This did not sit too well with the die-hards. But the tide could not be reversed.

Also in 1938, the congregation, numbering eighty-eight persons, was organized as an independent entity and officially named the Holland Marsh Christian Reformed Church. It was affiliated with the Christian Reformed Church in America, a denomination with Dutch roots established in 1857.

Tony Sneep is shown with his children Jean, Ann Marie, John and Neil in 1945.

A typical Sunday scene in Ansnorveldt in 1947.

Who's the first one to empty the bottle? The contest was part of the fun at the annual church picnic in 1947.

Rev. Balt again was one of the guests. His face had become a familiar one in the Marsh. The people looked forward to his visits. The consistory had even decided to pay half the cost of a heater for his Model-A Ford so that, as one resident reasoned, "he wouldn't freeze stiff before he got here."

The minister, on the other hand, must have had some mixed feelings about his trips to the land of mud. One time, while he motored down to conduct a communion service, his car became deeply mired in an ugly rut within sight of the Marsh. He bravely continued on foot, carrying the cup and plates on his shoulder.

There was strict discipline in those days. One church elder was reprimanded because he had taken his family and his neighbour's children to the hills for a Sunday afternoon picnic. This was deemed a wrongful activity for the Lord's Day. In future, he was told, he should set a better example.

The consistory also was greatly concerned at one point over a large number of youths travelling as far as eight miles to attend services at a gospel tabernacle. Worse still, some frequented movie houses in nearby towns. An attempt would be made to stop such liberal behaviour.

In 1940, when Holland was trying to cope with the Nazi invaders, the Dutch people in the Marsh had reason to smile: the congregation finally got its own pastor, Rev. Martin Schans of Redlands, California. A parsonage was completed just before his arrival. He was succeeded in 1946 by Rev. John van der Meer, formerly a missionary among the Navaho Indians and an army chaplain with the U.S. forces on the European front during the then recently-completed world conflict. The following year, he began to devote much effort to helping newly-arrived immigrants get settled in their new land. He even preached an extra sermon in Dutch for their benefit. He stayed until 1951.

The influx of immigrants, although welcomed with open arms, resulted in an acute overcrowding problem at the church. It wasn't unusual for stacking chairs to be placed in the aisle. There was only one solution: expand again. That took place in 1948 when the building was widened and lengthened and given a completely new front with a tower. The original structure had all but disappeared from view.

A few years later, the building again was bursting at the seams. So there were no misgivings when the people on the western side of the Marsh realized their goal of organizing a congregation with a church building of its own.

But the relief was temporary. Faced with no alternative, the Ansnorveldt congregation approved plans for a new church and parsonage across the road, on a three-acre parcel donated by Stoffer Oosterhuis. The $110,000 project was completed in late 1960.

"Today we say goodbye to the old building," Van Dyke said at the dedication. "It has been very dear to many of us. Within its walls, the word of God has been brought in roughly five thousand services, and a score of us have attended most of them."

The church played a cardinal role in the development of the Marsh as a community. In the early days, when difficulties abounded, its members hungered for strength and reassurance. They found in their Bible all that they needed to carry on. And further encouragement was provided through associating, especially on Sundays, with those of similar background who wrestled with identical problems and concerns. The church brought these people together and helped steer them through rough and uncertain times.

The companionship was most noticeable at the annual social outing at Innisfil Park on Lake Simcoe. "Once a year, we forgot about work," said Van Dyke. "We loaded up a big truck and went for a picnic. That was so enjoyable. Young and old took part in the games. There was a lunch. And while the children were splashing around in the water, the grownups sat in the shade and talked for hours. We really enjoyed the fellowship."

The Christian Reformed Church in Ansnorveldt.

Ansnorveldt once had a little Roman Catholic church, too, located across the road from where the general store used to be.

Curiously, none of the local history writings we consulted made any mention of it. Nor did the many people with whom we talked during our research of the community. A Dutch-language book entitled *Canada*, by J.W. Hofwijk, which was published in the Netherlands in the early 1950's, gave us the first clue in a one-sentence reference: "A few years ago a small church called St. James Chapel was built for the Catholics."

The simple frame structure, with a modest steeple on top, was built by a hired carpenter and a number of volunteers on a donated lot shortly after the Second World War when the Marsh became the end destination of many European immigrants. It was a mission of the Holy Martyrs of Japan Church in Bradford, then led by Father Melville Bolan.

Dutchman William Valenteyn, formerly of Kingston, Ontario, and one of the original inhabitants of the settlement, had been one of the main proponents of building a church in the Marsh strictly for the purpose of convenience. He lived only a few steps from the chapel, which made him an easy choice for assuming the caretaking duties. He swept away the muck in summer and the snow in winter and kept the dust to an acceptable level inside in all the seasons.

"When the weather was cold, he was at the church two hours before anyone else," recalled Nick Gasco, whose father John, a German-speaking Yugoslavian immigrant, first came to the Marsh in 1939. "That gave him plenty of time to get the oil burner going and warm up the place before the priest got here from Bradford. Then when everyone had left, he stayed behind to turn off the burner and tidy things up."

In the first years, between forty and fifty parishioners regularly went to St. James for mass. In time, however, the number dwindled, as more and more families preferred to go to Bradford, or some other nearby community, where the churches offered a wider fellowship through larger numbers and the existence of various societies.

As the Bradford parish grew, the heavy workload made it increasingly difficult for the pastor to continue making visits to

St. James Catholic Church in Ansnorveldt.

the Marsh. There were problems, too, with the building. Explained Gasco: "The church sat on a low spot in the field, which was very wet. And as a poor job had been done with the footings, the frost heaved it around a bit."

This combination of factors led to the closure of the mission in the 1960's. The building was then moved to its present location in the village of Sharon, east of Holland Landing. It was rebuilt and put back into service.

The Bradford area is also served well by a number of other churches of various denominations, including Anglican, Baptist, United and Presbyterian.

There's also another group with Dutch roots - a *Gereformeerde* congregation - which was organized in 1958. Its fifteen to twenty members rent space in the Presbyterian church in town for the alternating English and Dutch services which are conducted either by a lay person or a visiting minister.

~~~

Never Standing Still

At three o'clock in the morning on April 26, 1926, a train carrying Gerard and Anna Verkaik and their nine children screeched to a stop at the station in Chatham. The weary passengers, some of them hardly able to keep their eyes open, stepped out into the chilly air. A few minutes later, the locomotive built up steam and began to chug away, heading into the darkness.

The Verkaiks, standing alone on the platform, felt helpless. No one was there to greet them. Just off the boat, immigrants from the Haarlemmermeer, a reclaimed area, they had no place to go. All they knew was that they were in Chatham, their destination, one of the places to which newcomers were being steered.

The station master sauntered up to them, determined they were Dutch and then left to call Sam Winter, a Dutchman he knew. Before long, the entire family was bedded down on Winter's floor. For a few fleeting hours, they were dead to the world.

"First thing in the morning," said Peter, fourteen years old then, "Dad went looking for a house. He found one at a reasonable rent, bought some used furniture and moved us in."

Not too many hours had passed in the new abode before the senior Verkaik began to itch in a few awkward places. Son Harry had the same complaint. Soon more members of the family were furiously scratching here, there and everywhere. The house, it turned out, was infested with bedbugs - flat, reddish-brown insects that consume only blood.

Anna Verkaik fought a losing battle with them. Fed up, she and the others packed their belongings and moved out to the country. This turned out to be to their advantage; most of the available jobs were on the farms. They worked here and there, and even share-cropped tobacco, all the while bringing in enough money for the food and the rent.

In 1930, with the Depression under way, Father Verkaik bought a farm of one

Peter Verkaik stokes his peppermint still.

Above: Mr. and Mrs. Gerard Verkaik

Nellie Verkaik pays a visit to the outhouse, a common fixture before people could afford the installation of indoor conveniences.

Peter Verkaik

The reports filtering in from Holland Marsh were too rosy to be ignored. Father Verkaik perceived an opportunity for his boys. Accordingly, in 1935, he and Peter drove up for an inspection. They were so impressed with the flatness of the land, which reminded them of Holland, and the black soil, which looked so rich, that they immediately inquired about the availability of land. Peter Greyn steered them to a farmer on the west side, Matthew Brandon, who had expressed a desire to sell the back part of his acreage near the north canal.

"Mr. Brandon was on his tractor, working the land," said Peter. "We told him what we were interested in. We were told that ninety acres of undeveloped, first-class muck soil was for sale for $2,000. Dad offered him $1,800. Mr. Brandon then pulled away, went around his field and came back to us. He would not lower his price. So we left."

After driving a few miles on the road back to Chatham, Peter suddenly stepped on the brakes and said: "If that property is not worth $2,000, then it's not worth $1,800 either. On the other hand if it's worth $1,800, then it's also worth $2,000." Father agreed. They turned around and headed for the man on the tractor.

A lot of hard work was in store for the Verkaiks. That same fall, they built a two-room shack, twelve feet by eighteen feet, which served as temporary living quarters while they dug two miles of drainage ditches by hand. They were back in early spring to break up their large expanse with the help of an oil-driven tractor that had a bad habit of setting the coating of fine dust on fire. A pail of water hung on the machine for ready use during such emergencies.

hundred acres. His goal was to pay back the borrowed funds as quickly as possible, even though money was scarce. He grew some extra crops, such as tobacco, strawberries and early tomatoes, and got his sons, who drove a truck, to sell the harvest to stores throughout southern Ontario.

"His mind was always full of schemes to keep us busy, especially in winter, and thus rake in some money," recalled Peter. "One time, when there was little work to go around, he got the idea of acquiring knitting machines for making socks. That's right, he wanted us to make socks. But that didn't go over well because we had no desire to become machine operators. Then there was the idea of buying cattle and hogs - bulls, boars and even rams - butchering them and selling the meat to foreigners in Windsor. The price was right, so the people didn't complain about the meat being too tough. We made $600 in one winter and became the richest people on our concession road."

Wagons loaded with freshly-harvested vegetables leave the Verkaik fields.

The Holland River: fresh and sparkling in early spring.

"The area was still largely undeveloped," said Peter. "There were no roads or bridges. The dike was merely humps of dirt taken out of the canal; it hadn't been bulldozed yet for the road on top. We placed some logs across the canal to create access to the outer world, particularly Bradford. All the bags of seed potatoes and fertilizer were carried across those logs. With careful balancing, no one had the misfortune of falling in. The horses simply swam to the other side. In the summer, a bridge was built and the logs were abandoned."

After a few years of moving his equipment back and forth between his farm in Chatham and the one in Holland Marsh, Father Verkaik decided he had enough. The arrangement had been cumbersome and counter-productive. So he sold his land in the Marsh to sons Jake, Harry and Peter. They took over in the spring of 1939.

It was still a time of experimentation - of determining what could flourish in the muck and also be acceptable to the marketplace. The Verkaik brothers, while staying with the main crops, decided to set aside some land for peppermint plants from which oil, used as an ingredient for various products, including medicine candies and distillery goods, could be extracted.

It took a year for the stringy roots to develop to a length of up to four feet and with sprouts every four to six inches. The next year, they were dug up and replanted in rows a yard apart. The plants attained a height of twenty-four to thirty inches and looked not unlike fields of alfalfa, hay or clover.

"It was my job to get the peppermint thing going," explained Peter. "I manufactured a planter, a two-seater, to get the roots into the ground. It made a furrow, the person on the planter put in the roots and then a small scraper or plough covered everything up. It worked very well. I was rather proud of myself."

He had obtained the parts from scrapyards. Many other growers did the same thing in those days. The weirdest-looking contraptions, such as tractors made from discarded cars and

Peter Verkaik is happy with the abundance of his crop.

trucks, made an appearance. They were a far cry from the later equipment, especially adapted for the spongy soil. But they did their job - and exemplified the ingenuity and resourcefulness of the people who had come to the Marsh.

When the peppermint crop was ready, Peter put a bale of it in the trunk of his car and drove to Decatur, Michigan, to seek the advice of a friend, Hoekstra by name, who ran a similar farming operation.

"Steam produced by a boiler had to be used to get the oil out of the crop. In other words, it had to be cooked out. Specially-made tanks held the peppermint hay. The steam would go in and come out, taking the oil with it. A separator and condenser were used to isolate the oil from the steam."

Peter's bale was placed in a tank. A test run determined that it contained enough oil. Encouraged, he bought two used tanks, ten feet high and eight feet wide, and some ancillary equipment. Before long, a still was in operation in the Marsh, emitting a peppermint odour that was detected by noses miles away. Wormwood, a plant whose oil was used for appetitive purposes, also was processed.

"The peppermint oil was sold by the pound," said Peter. "We didn't grow a large acreage of the crop as it was an experiment to see if it would be profitable. Well, it was a lot of work and the results were such that it did not pay. We sold the still to someone in the Grand Bend muck region, northwest of Chatham, where it was used for a number of years."

Two years after taking over the market garden, with Canada embroiled in the world conflict and with the demand for Marsh vegetables on the upswing, the brothers bought another three hundred acres which had been put on the market for tax arrears. Parts of this acquisition were sold to brother George and Dutchmen Art van Dyke and Albert van Dyke.

Peter, who married Nellie Rupke, a member of the well-known Marsh clan, and had seven children, was full of memories of the early years behind the dike when we visited him at the summer home on Lake Simcoe.

He chuckled when he told the story of two young labourers, paid fifteen cents an hour, who went on strike for three days in a futile attempt to get an extra five cents. He grinned when he recalled brother Harry losing his wallet with $150 in it while he was sitting on a potato digger, the fruitless searching that followed, and then someone knocking on the door two weeks later and announcing unexpectedly: "I found it!" There was a hint of a frown when he talked about the experiments that didn't live up to expectations, including the growing of bird seed.

But he was all smiles again as he recalled the hot, humid day when a girl working in the lettuce patch caused a small sensation by removing her brassiere to cool off. "I didn't know what to do."

Peter later branched out on his own, buying two hundred and fifty acres of marshland near Beeton, west of the Marsh. He put in his own drainage system. Over the years, this farm developed into a productive enterprise. Its vegetables, plus large quantities purchased from other growers, were shipped to many points, including Canada's Atlantic provinces.

With bigger things in mind, he sold the farm and, together with three sons, bought around six hundred acres of muck land near Eustis, Florida. They all worked hard to get everything in shape. Then the torrential rains came - twenty-three inches in three weeks - and all the plants were drowned. As a result of this hapless experience, the land was sold. Peter then turned to another enterprise: the establishment of a seed business, J.C. Canner's Seed Company, specializing in the sale of carrot seed to growers in the United States and Canada.

"I don't want to sit in an easy chair and watch television all day," he said. "I'm at the age when I should be doing that. But as long as I've got my health, I want to keep busy. I've always been that way."

~~~

Their Own School

An important question faced the settlers of 1934: where could their children go to school?

They determined that the nearest public school was at Amsterdam, a hamlet outside the Marsh and, via shortcuts, a two-mile walking distance away. This school, however, was in another township - East Gwillimbury - which precluded the children from being enrolled there.

The next closest school was at Glenville, a hamlet on what is now Highway 9 south of the Marsh. It was 2 1/2 miles away, requiring the youngsters to climb a series of steep hills along Concession 3, the road leading from the settlement. The parents could envisage their children being lost in a snowstorm on their way home from school and succumbing to the cold darkness.

Despite such worries, some of the children did go to Glenville. The others simply stayed home and did chores. A provincial law which compelled them to attend school did not seem to be strictly enforced. But when the really cold weather set in, practically no one ventured across the lonely stretch of the highlands.

The bottom line of all this was manifest: Ansnorveldt needed a school of its own.

The authorities agreed. A one-room public school, S.S. No. 86 King, was built on a one-acre lot at the far end of the row of houses which had been donated by the owners, Nolan and Green of Bradford. It was completed in time for the start of the new school year in September, 1935.

"It didn't cost the taxpayers all that much," said John van Dyke. "During its construction, there was only one paid labourer - the carpenter, Tony Sneep. The men of the community pitched in with volunteer labour and did a lot of the work."

Many dignitaries attended the official opening on September 23, including the Ontario minister of education, Dr. L.J. Simpson, and the Dutch consul-general, A. Nordheimer. John Snor, who had played a key role in bringing the school idea to reality, was chairman of the program.

The first teacher was Miss Eileen Nolan of Bradford, who looked after all eight grades and later even had two students in the ninth grade. She was adored by young and old.

The staunch Calvinists in the settlement didn't really mind that she was Roman Catholic. "She never pushed her religion on the children," explained Van Dyke. The parents seemed to be satisfied with the quality of education and the pleasant atmosphere. But all that changed.

Carpenter Tony Sneep nailed together many structures in Ansnorveldt, including the public school.

The public school is about to be officially opened in 1935.

"When other people, non-Dutch, moved into the district, a movement appeared within our own group to set up our own school. The board of the public school at first consisted mostly of our own people - I was on it too - but later not one of us was left. We were losing control. The school also became overfull and the quality of education suffered."

Moreover, some parents couldn't get along well with Miss Nolan's replacement, a male and also a Roman Catholic. There was also talk that an extension of the building would be required and that the taxpayers would have to foot the $5,000 bill.

The Dutch in the community figured the time was ripe for establishing their own school. It wouldn't be a public one; it would be a Christian school, which would offer the same basic education, but with one fundamental difference - with the whole development of the child in mind, the instruction would be based on the teachings of the Bible. Enrolment wouldn't be restricted to the Dutch or those of the Reformed faith.

Most of the adults in the settlement had attended Christian schools in Holland. Deep down, they harboured a distrust of the public school system, regarding it as secular and possibly frought with danger for the spiritual health of their children.

A school society was set up. At a meeting, attended by

This memento of the official opening of the public school, signed by the guests, is a cherished possession of John Snor's offspring.

twenty people, it was decided to go ahead with a separate school. The year was 1942.

One of the prime movers was the pastor of the village church, Rev. Martin Schans, who had some experience in launching Christian schools in the United States. Now that the parents had made up their minds, he would attempt to find out whether their school taxes could be diverted to their project. Many believed - and hoped - that there would be no difficulty with this.

In time, however, Rev. Schans had to convey some bad news: "We had been told and were in hopes that we could use the school tax, which we had been paying toward the maintenance of the public school, for our own Christian school. But we found that we were mistaken. The Roman Catholic Church has that privilege for its parochial schools, but no other religious group has." This peculiar education policy dated back to the time when most of the non-native people in Canada were either British or French.

Although there were no restrictions on starting a private school, the financial plight loomed large. With no tax dollars or grants to back them, could the handful of people afford such an undertaking? A lot of money would be needed to buy land, erect a building, furnish and maintain it, pay a teacher and acquire supplies.

Undaunted, the parents decided to push ahead. At the annual church picnic in August, money was collected and pledges were made. A door-to-door canvass also brought results.

With cash in hand, the school board searched for a site and found three acres available for $150. Tony Sneep, the master builder, came up with detailed plans for the school, including a woodshed and a privy. King Township, however, refused to grant a building permit, considering a private school non-essential during the wartime shortage of building materials.

An interior view of the room behind the church.

Not wanting to waste any more time, the board sought permission from the church to rent the small consistory room for use as a classroom. This presented no problem. The room even was enlarged somewhat - without a permit.

A teacher was needed. Walter Horlings, the treasurer then, recalled the efforts to find one in a hurry: "We heard there was a Mrs. de Jong in Sarnia, who had been a teacher in the Netherlands; her husband was in the Dutch army. I had to bring a load of vegetables to Chatham, so Rev. Schans could come along in the truck to meet her

The church's consistory room was enlarged to accommodate the pupils.

Above: Rev. Martin Schans

During the warm months, there were lots of chores to be done after school, including the gathering of firewood and the peeling of potatoes.

for an interview. I loaded the truck in late afternoon, ready for an early start the next morning. I still had to rush to a service station on Highway 11 to fill the tank because they were not allowed to sell gas after 6 p.m. On my way there, somebody's poodle ran in front of the truck and got under the wheel. Poor doggie was as dead as a doornail. The next day, Rev. Schans and I made the seven-hour trip to Chatham. A close friend of Rev. Schans, Rev. Leonard Trip, was willing to drive the fifty miles to Sarnia. We approached Mrs. de Jong, but she thought she was not capable of teaching the language of the land. All that trip for nothing."

Horlings then suggested another name on the short list: Jacob Uitvlugt of Chatham, who had been afflicted with recurring bouts of tuberculosis, which at one time had even threatened his deportation, but who was now well on the way to full recovery.

Uitvlugt, a native of Nieuwe Pekela, in the province of Groningen, had no formal training as a teacher. He was schooled as a sailor and served as an officer on a merchant ship which sailed to and from points in South America. In September, 1927, he and his bride, Geertje, had set out for Canada to rejoin his parents, who had emigrated to Chatham three years earlier. The elder Uitvlugts later moved to the U.S.

One day, the postman brought Uitvlugt a handwritten letter, in Dutch, from Simon Winter, secretary of the school society in Holland Marsh. "At our general society meeting this evening," it stated, "you were unanimously approved of to become the principal/teacher of the school we hope to open soon ... Your salary will be $85 per month with contract renewable on a yearly basis... You will be provided with a rent-free home which has a large garden... Your salary will also be paid during the two vacation months of July and August... This will set your salary at $1,020 a year... The number of students that will be attending from grades one through eight is approximately eighteen... We would like the school to open in January, 1943..."

On their way to the Marsh in early 1943 to take up the new post, Mr. and Mrs. Uitvlugt and their three children ran into snow and slippery roads. Their vehicle, a Durant, landed upside down in a ditch somewhere near Woodstock. It was a writeoff. They managed to get to Hamilton, where they stayed with friends, Mr. and Mrs. John van der Vliet, and finally made it to their destination one week behind schedule.

Some of the original pupils.

Jacob Uitvlugt

The growth of the Christian school in Ansnorveldt is reflected in this group photo of the early 1950's.

Their home was still being fumigated for bedbugs, so they were the guests of the minister and his wife for about six weeks.

The grand opening of the school took place on February 15. In his address to the parents, Uitvlugt said: "By the grace of God, I am standing here before you today to begin the work of teaching your children. In this moment I feel as if I am standing at the foot of a towering mountain, and as I begin to climb, it is with my weakness, but with God's strength. I know that the path up the mountain may be steep and dangerous, but I go with God, and I do not fear."

The Ladies Aid of the church had donated $60 for a stove and a clock. The board had set a budget of $1,500 for the coming year, and parents had enrolled twenty-two children. The first parent-controlled, Calvinistic Christian school in Canada was off and running, even though the textbooks hadn't arrived yet and the pupils had to make do with only paper and pencils.

Uitvlugt's daughter, Kitty, recalled: "The privileges of attending a Christian school were felt immediately as we began that day and every day thereafter with prayer, hymn-singing and Bible stories. Materially we lacked a few things, but spiritually we were overwhelmingly rich."

Horlings remembered the reaction of outsiders.

"Some were angry, scared that our taxes would go to our school, the same as with the Roman Catholic schools, which would mean higher taxes for them. Others thought we would teach only Dutch. On the other hand, I also know of one elderly couple who would not contribute to the Christian school unless we taught Dutch."

Busing the pupils over long distances was a real headache in those days, mainly because the scarcity of funds gave rise to poor equipment and numerous mechanical breakdowns. The first vehicle, an old station wagon, was operated by John Miedema. Later, a second-hand bus, with Sierk Rupke at the wheel, huffed and puffed up and down the country roads.

The school society became incorporated in October, 1947, enabling it to borrow $4,000 from a trust company for the construction of its own building on the previously-acquired lot across the road. Two old army barracks purchased in nearby Newmarket were converted, with the help of much volunteer labour, into a three-room school, complete with an office and indoor washrooms. The enrolment had grown to eighty-two pupils. Miss Emma Knapper became the teacher for the first four grades while Uitvlugt remained as principal and taught the senior grades.

Uitvlugt, by the way, later upgraded his formal education by attending summer courses at Calvin College in Grand

The school made out of army barracks.

Teacher and pupils take time out from class for informal photos.

Rapids, Michigan. He would remain in the Marsh until 1957, when he moved to Bowmanville, east of Toronto, to launch a new Christian school there.

The influx into Canada of thousands upon thousands of Dutch immigrants in the late 1940's and early 1950's had resulted in a big demand for the provision of Christian education. The Marsh even got a second school. It was opened in 1955 on the west side, thus providing some relief for the inadequate fa-

cilities at Ansnorveldt. The year before, Hurricane Hazel had struck the Marsh in full fury, inundating it all, and leaving the wood-frame school in the settlement water-logged and beyond repair. In 1957, a new brick school replaced the barracks. More classrooms were added later, mainly as a result of parents in Newmarket sending their children to the Marsh.

In the early 1980's, the two boards in the Marsh amalgamated and the school in the village was enlarged, complete with a gym, to eliminate the need for two buildings. Accordingly, the school on the west side was closed.

The public schoolhouse in Ansnorveldt no longer exists. Centralization of education facilities put it out of use as an elementary school in 1963. For years after that, it served as the meeting place of the Calvinist Cadet Corps of the church. In May, 1985, a tornado that roared through the Marsh shifted the building off its foundation. It was subsequently demolished, despite the wishes of some people to have it restored for historical reasons, and a new cadet hall was built on the site.

So a lot of changes have taken place, except one: the parents are still waiting for the government to enact legislation for directing tax money to the school. In the meantime, they, like

Like their parents had done in Holland, children have cleared a section of the ice-covered canal for an afternoon of skating.

The Holland Marsh District Christian School in Ansnorveldt.

the settlers of 1934, have to pay a yearly fee for their children's education while their tax levies are being used for the support of the public system.

The Holland Marsh District Christian School now consists of twelve classrooms and has an enrolment of nearly three hundred students.

It was not until 1950 that the Roman Catholic students in Bradford area also got a school of their own.

Before then, the ones from the Marsh attended the public school in Ansnorveldt. There they received religious instruction once a week - one hour on Wednesdays, after school was dismissed at four o' clock - from the priest who served the parish in Bradford.

"If Father Bolan was five minutes late, we'd be gone, on our way home," chuckled Nick Gasco. "Then he would drive down the roads, round us up and take us back to the school."

The two-room St. Mary's Queen of Martyrs School at Frederick and Barrie Streets in Bradford was opened for fifty-three students, mostly of Slavic origin, under the supervision of Father Francis McGinn and three sisters of the Ursuline Order.

The whole Catholic community pitched in to help the nuns with building and equipping the school. It was a busy time, as construction of the St. Mary's Convent of Assumption was also under way. The men contributing their building skills and the women held showers, offering kitchen utensils, linen and foodstuffs, especially vegetables.

The first Christmas concert at St. Mary's reflected the ethnic makeup of the student body. It featured carols in Latin, English, Dutch, Polish and German.

Two years after the school opened, the student population had more than doubled, the result of many new immigrant families settling in the area, including the Marsh. Two classrooms were added. But the overcrowding problem didn't go away, and it was necessary to build two more classrooms two years later. The school grew until it could hold no more - at one time even the auditorium was partitioned into classrooms - and in 1961 St. Charles School in West Gwillimbury was opened, which eased the congestion temporarily. Another new school, Mary of the Incarnation, was built in Bradford in 1975.

And on and on the story goes - a story of unflagging growth, of the community pulling together to meet the many challenges, of the development of a local system that gives children of varied backgrounds an opportunity to receive a solid education in an environment where Christian values are appreciated.

~~~

Fans of Royalty

While the Marsh was showing signs of promise, Professor William Day was having a rough time personally.

His syndicate eventually lost much of its land because of staggering tax arrears. And in 1937, he had to give up his remaining land through bankruptcy.

A heart attack killed him on a hot summer day in 1938 while he was working on a small, rented parcel which he had called KingGwillimBrad Gardens, an anagram of the three local municipalities.

"I was on my own lot, number five, and the professor was on lot eight," recalled Tom Fuller, a former employee of Day's, who later started his own gardening operation. "I saw Bill Day, the elder of two sons, come roaring out of the field, saying something was wrong. He had been helping his father plant celery. The professor's death touched everyone in the Marsh. It was sad when you think of all the work he'd done for so long and yet he had

A stone monument in Professor Day's honour stands in front of the municipal building in Bradford.

been so poor. Especially if you think of how much money has been made in the Marsh from 1923 to now. It's in the billions."

Other growers struggled too, of course. But those who had not over-extended themselves with debt were able to scrape by. Every penny brought in by the harvest was accounted for.

"We were dirt poor," said Jan Rupke's son, John. "We had no money to spare at all. It's no wonder that the older children had to leave home, go away from the Marsh, to get a job and bring in some of the badly-needed cash. Quite a few of the young girls went to Hamilton to do housework. They sent their pay to their parents."

During the off-season, John and his brother, Bill, provided the money for groceries. John worked for a florist in Stoney Creek, near Hamilton, ten hours a day, six days a week, at $1 a

day. Bill was an assistant cook at the Eaton's department store in Hamilton and earned slightly more. John's work experience also included peddling groceries door to door on behalf of a Dutchman who ran a store in Hamilton.

Simon Winter once gave a graphic example of the plight of the Marsh people:

"One woman wanted so badly to go to church. But she couldn't bring herself around to it because she didn't have a cent to spare for the offering. Then she came up with an idea: she dug up a few of the violets that were growing outside her place, made up four little trays and placed them for sale at the roadside. A car went by, a rare occurrence in the Marsh. The lady driver spotted the flowers, stopped and bought all the trays at fifteen cents apiece. Needless to say, every penny was given to the church."

Notwithstanding the hardships, the early settlers were able to keep their heads above water. They were obstinately sticking it out, knowing that life outside the Marsh was difficult too. Moreover, they had faith in themselves and in the viability of their fledgling businesses. They were convinced that one day things would turn around and that prosperity would be ushered in.

As each year went by, and the crops became more bountiful and the number of happy customers also increased, the confidence of the growers attained new heights. The little village grew; houses were built on the other side of the road. Even the church, as was noted earlier, had to be enlarged.

The houses, immaculately kept and even landscaped to some extent, stood out conspicuously in comparison with most other dwellings on the Marsh. Many among the latter were suitable for summer occupancy only. With production confined to eight months of the year, there was a large floating population. Neither the owners nor the inhabitants of the substandard housing - mere shacks in some instances - were interested in neatness and upkeep.

The Dutch of Ansnorveldt, on the other hand, were year-round residents. Outsiders seemed impressed with what these people were accomplishing. They admired the stark determination and the strong sense of community, the latter quality exemplified by the desire of the settlers to invest their assets in the immediate surroundings.

The Marsh had clearly shown the need for a selected type of settler - and the Dutch filled the bill.

In time, their hard work would be rewarded with larger profits. Some would increase their holdings and improve their houses, even adding on extensions. And a few of the sons, ready to start on their own, would move to other parts of the Marsh.

Ted van der Goot's blue eyes lit up when he showed a framed photograph of a little boy biting into a rusk, called a 'beschuit', a regular item on the breakfast tables in Holland.

"That's me. A newspaper took it in 1938 when we had a big party at the public school in the village to celebrate the birth of Beatrix who is now the Dutch queen. That was a big event. Everyone went."

The aniseed-covered rusks, also traditional fare for guests at get-togethers after births, were a big hit with the youngsters. The grownups got their thrills by lustily singing 'Wilhelmus,' the Dutch national anthem, and other songs they knew so well and loved. They even congratulated each other.

The Dutch in the Marsh held their royalty close to their heart, as indeed did most of the immigrants who had settled

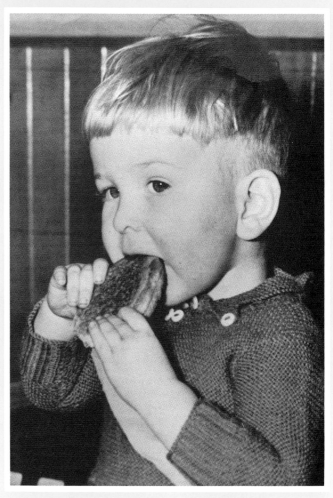

Little Ted van der Goot samples a 'beschuit' during celebrations in Ansnorveldt.

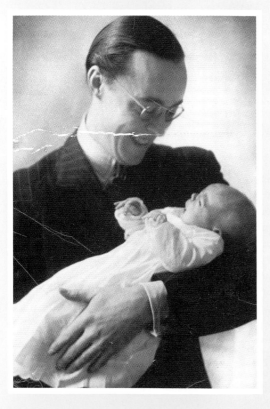

Prince Bernhard shows off daughter Beatrix, born on January 31, 1938.

elsewhere. For years, they followed the custom of hauling out the Dutch flag on royal birthdays, and everyone sported a bit of orange, the colour of the royal house.

The following recollection of an immigrant who had settled elsewhere in Ontario can be applied to the experiences of the first Marsh settlers as well: "On August 31, it was 'Koninginnedag', the day we celebrated Wilhelmina's birthday in Holland. So my husband asked the farmer if he could get off work early. At four o'clock, the party started. The girls put on white dresses with orange sashes and ribbons; the boys white shorts, white shirts and orange caps. Two other Dutch families came. First we had a parade. Dad in front with the trumpet. Around the house and the barn to the garden where everybody sang 'Wilhelmus' loud enough to set the birds flying. Then in the house for supper. After supper, our Canadian sponsors came. Everybody played games, sang songs and told stories. Our Canadian friends agreed that these Dutch people sure knew how to have good parties."

Early on, a cluster of residents just north of the settlement had decided to call a nearby sideroad the Juliana Road in honour of the crown princess, Queen Wilhelmina's only child, and a favourite among the immigrants. The idea caught on quickly. Bernhard, Juliana's husband, was recognized, and so were Wilhelmina and her mother Emma.

The names are still there, reminding residents and visitors alike of the area's Dutch roots. There's a minor flaw, however: Bernhard is spelled 'Bernhardt' and Wilhelmina is shown as 'Wilhelmena' on the road signs.

"That doesn't really bother me," remarked a Toronto businessman of Dutch descent. "Whenever I want to get away from it all, I take a drive to the Marsh. I love it there; it reminds me of Holland. That matters most."

One day in the early 1940's, the Dutch community was abuzz with the news that two of its young women had been selected to serve as chambermaids for Princess Juliana who then was living in Rockcliffe Park, a suburb of Ottawa, far away from the dangers and miseries that the German war machine had brought to her homeland and much of the rest of Europe.

But the honour that everyone felt at that time pales in comparison with the jubilation that had greeted the happy tidings of the birth of Juliana's first daughter in 1938.

The blessed event was worthy of a gala celebration. There would be what the Dutch call an 'Oranjefeest', a day of festivities in honour of the House of Orange. A committee consisting of Abraham Havinga, Jan Rupke and Cor Sneep was set up to arrange the program.

A carnival atmosphere prevailed on Monday, February 21, a few weeks after the birth. There was no school that day, and the adults put their work aside. Everyone took part in the merrymaking from early afternoon, when the activities started, to late at night, when the last firecracker burst over the public schoolhouse.

One of the road signs in the Dutch settlement.

Young and old displayed a touch of orange. The red, white and blue of the Dutch flag and the Union Jack, which was used widely before Canada had a flag of its own, were the other colours that were conspicuous wherever one looked.

A parade along the settlement's road got the events under way. The marshall, Henry Turkstra, led the procession on a bay horse which was draped in a large Union Jack. Next came a standard-bearer. The committee members, looking dignified with their ribbons and top hats, and most of the inhabitants, noisily blowing kazoos, followed in behind. Everyone headed for the schoolhouse where the rest of the program would be held, out of the cold.

There were games, periods of song, recitations and feasting - including the distribution of the rusks which little Ted enjoyed so much. Children were given prizes for the best reading in Dutch. The most exciting and amusing of the games was balloon-trapping by ten boys. Cow-bladders were filled with air and one was tied by a short string to the left ankle of each boy. Then each tried to protect himself and break the others' balloons.

There were serious moments too. One news report of the festivities stated: "They also prayed. The program was interspersed with the reading of psalms, singing of hymns, and short prayers by the older men."

One of the coveted prizes was a reproduction of a painting of William of Orange, the founder of the royal house. The other sought-after prizes were $25, $15 and $10 in cash, donated by John Snor, which were to be awarded to the owners of the best decorated houses in the settlement.

The residents had been encouraged to embellish their dwellings in a royal theme. Entire families enthusiastically immersed themselves in the challenging task of creating an eye-catching entry. Neighbour tried to outdo neighbour, employing scarce materials to the best advantage. The result was a unique and colourful display of adoration for baby Beatrix and her family.

Simon Winter placed first with his royal family tree, made out of twigs and enhanced with orange ribbon, that graced the front of his house. Jan Rupke took second spot with his presentation of a Dutch double door emblazoned with a stork and the words *Het is volbracht* (It is fulfilled).

Havinga, who collected third prize, told a reporter: "The royal family in Holland has been good to the people, and they love their rulers. We are Canadians now, and we love Canada, but we share their joy and celebrate with them. We could not be good Canadians if we were not good Dutchmen."

The Dutch residents of the Marsh, by the way, are still waiting for a member of the royal family to drop in and say hello.

Henrietta Prins, Gerald Rupke and Annie Barselaar show off their Dutch costumes.

ANSNORVELD CELEBRATES CHRISTENING OF HOLLAND'S NEW

The press covered the festivities in the Marsh with pictorial features. This interesting display shows Jan Rupke trying to impress one of the younger set, Jackie Turkstra; a number of young ladies admiring a Dutch flag; committee members Abraham Havinga , Jan Rupke and Cor Sneep; young and old making a lot of noise with their kazoos, and Henry Turkstra leading the parade. The Dutch residents of the Marsh, by the way, are still waiting for a member of the royal family to drop in and say hello.

~~~

It's a Big Business

In the early years, rugged individualism stood out when it came to marketing the crops. Despite the camaraderie and the willingness to help each other, every grower seemed to be in competition with his neighbour in the search for precious dollars. It was considered shrewd dealing to harvest ahead of the others and then speed to Toronto to capture the highest price.

Of course, such rivalry was to no one's benefit in the long run. A united effort was needed. Some growers who produced crops of excellent quality didn't have the business instinct and the time to market them to the fullest monetary advantage. Besides, only a combined strategy could promote this new area as a producer of the finest lettuce, carrots and other vegetables to be found in Ontario and possibly all of Canada.

An attempt was made in 1936-37 to form a united front. Some 130 growers - yes, the number had grown substantially since the arrival of the Dutch settlers - formed the Holland Marsh Vegetable Growers Co-operative Association. The goal was co-operative marketing of crops and buying of seeds, fertilizers and implements. Some of the produce ended up as far as Montreal. Still, a self-centred attitude seemed to prevail.

A few years later, the Dutch Growers Association was set up for the particular interests of the increasing number of Dutchmen in the Marsh. It packed lettuce and celery and dealt with wholesalers. However, its salesmen didn't sell everything and there was some dispute about what to do with the leftover crop. As a result, some growers began to sell independently as before. The organization folded after two years.

Many growers remained largely dependent on local markets. This meant selling their produce at dilapidated roadside stands or through the unpopular money-grabbing commission houses in Toronto. Some of the lucky ones secured contracts with grocery stores and even national supermarket chains. During the harvest, the odd retailer even drove to the Marsh to hand-pick his supply.

Sometimes it was just impossible for a grower to find a market. Overabundance was usually to blame. The result was the dumping of vegetables, a heartbreaking experience. Cold-storage facilities had not come on the scene yet to any appreciable extent.

It wasn't until after the Second World War that a definite

The 'polder' landscape near Bradford.

The Holland River Gardens plant on Bradford's outskirts.

swing took place away from the harmful competition. Larger co-operatives and produce and storage firms were established, encouraging mechanization, sophisticated marketing techniques and increasingly greater production.

In 1946, the Bradford Co-operative Storage Limited was formed by 150 of the Marsh's five hundred growers who paid $100 a share. A large cold-storage plant was built on the eastern outskirts of Bradford, with assistance from the federal and provincial governments, permitting vegetables to be placed on the market in good condition throughout the early winter months. The market expanded from Toronto and Montreal to places spread as far as Halifax, Nova Scotia, and Saskatoon, Saskatchewan.

The co-op is still being used for storage, but not cold stor-

The formation of the Bradford Co-operative Storage Limited in 1946 was a sure sign that the Marsh was flourishing.

age. This change came about when it was decided not to proceed with a complete, and costly, overhaul required by new government regulations.

Over the years, other attempts have been made to sell particular crops co-operatively. The lettuce growers had visions of less vexation and more business. So did the onion people. In the end, however, marketing boards were given the cold shoulder by the predominant sector which had determined that greater profits could be reaped by wheeling and dealing on an individual basis.

Also in 1946, just in time for the harvest season, the Holland River Gardens Company Limited set up a $105,000 ice-packing plant near the co-op. Founded by three Horlings brothers - Walter, Harry and George - the firm washed, packed and iced the vegetables produced on its own acreage as well as on those of others, and sold everything wholesale.

George, the youngest and the marketing expert - each brother had his own specialization - had become convinced that there was always a ready market, somewhere in Canada, for the quality products produced by the Marsh. The key was to get them to the dinner tables "harvest fresh." He sold his brothers on the idea of packing vegetables in powdered ice, thus keeping them fresh until they reached distant customers.

The results were gratifying. People fell in love with the packaged food, all ready for the salad bowl or the dinner pot. Within two years, it was offered in every province, along the eastern seaboard of the United States and even in faraway Hawaii. Yes, the Marsh was gaining a wide reputation for excellence. In New York City, for example, the lettuce earned a premium of fifty cents a case over the best American variety.

George told an interviewer in 1949: "Our problem is not over-production, but under-production. This company has a standing order to supply Detroit with 1,500 cases of lettuce a day, when and if we can guarantee shipment. Then there is New York City - we could ship a trainload of vegetables a day to this huge consumer market equalling that of all Canada. It is only twenty-two hours trucking distance from the Marsh, whereas our nearest big competitor - California - is three thousand miles away. Here again, lack of continuous supply is the obstacle. With sufficient production, our markets are unlimited."

Others took note of the success. In rapid succession, a number of other packing plants sprung up in the town: Federal Farms Ltd., Superior Packers, Hochreiters, Bradford Shippers, Dominion Fruit, International Fruit Distributor Ltd., United Farms and Molokachs.

In addition, some of the larger growers did their own preparation of vegetables for their private contracts and operated their own storage plants.

The wide open spaces fronting on Highway 11 in east Bradford and backed by railway tracks soon became a continuous row of industrial buildings. Large trucks pulled up at the

loading platforms. Refrigerated railway cars also got their share of the business. The value of the shipments soared into the millions.

In 1948-49, for instance, the CNR transported no fewer than 1,036 carloads of vetegables valued at close to $7 million. What a stark contrast to the first year, 1930, when the thirty-seven acres under cultivation brought in around $26,000.

The processing plants, though relentless rivals, adopted a wise pattern to lessen duplication. Holland River Gardens, for example, specialized in variety and was an experimenter in new ideas. Not only did it pack practically every variety of vegetable grown in the Marsh, it featured peeled and sliced potatoes, treated against discolouration, a favourite of hotels and restaurants. Federal Farms, on the other hand, specialized in volume, with emphasis on potatoes, carrots and onions.

The three Horlings brothers - another brother, Bill, operated his own gardens - farmed three hundred acres, placing them among the largest landowners in the Marsh. They provided a hundred jobs in the fields and a hundred in their plant. To en-

The Harm Horlings family prior to emigration.

The packaged vegetables were shipped to an expanding market, providing hundreds of jobs on the production lines.

The Marsh growers parade their trucks in 1948 as part of a publicity day at the Bradford Co-operative.

sure a supply of good labourers, they sponsored thirty immigrant families, some of whom remained in the Marsh after deciding to strike out on their own.

Holland River Gardens, flourishing and expanding, exemplified what a combination of good ideas, entrepreneurial spirit and hard work could achieve. Like other early settlers, the Horlings had started from scratch.

In 1926, the family, recently arrived in Canada, rented a two hundred-acre farm near Chatham and grew sugarbeets, then a major crop in that area. This venture, however, turned out to be shortlived.

"It really was too soon for us to run a farm," explained Walter, the oldest brother. "We were lost with it. We were used to working with fine soil, not the heavy kind we had on that farm. It was a very wet year and we had trouble getting the beets out of the ground. This discouraged us, and we gave up after a year."

Walter later bought an old truck and employed it to the fullest. The sugar company in Chatham paid him $1.25 an hour for hauling beets from the farms to the plant. There wasn't much other work around. By this time, the Depression had set in.

"But I always managed to get by, earning a dollar here and a dollar there," he said. "I was never on relief."

He first heard about Holland Marsh in 1934 from friends who had been there. His curiosity was aroused further when he heard that Albert Biemold, who had lived in the Chatham area, had settled there with government assistance. Well, he decided to have a look for himself. Perhaps here was an opportunity for him to get back to his first love - farming.

"I was impressed with what I saw. In Chatham, we couldn't grow cauliflower in the summer because of the rain. Well, they were growing cauliflower in the Marsh. The type of soil was more to my liking."

Walter paid $300 down for fifteen acres of partly cultivated land. He moved to the Marsh the following year, spending his nights in a sixteen by sixteen-foot shack which he had trucked from Chatham along with six tons of fertilizer.

"That first year was a big disappointment. I didn't know enough about farming in the Marsh. Also, there was no market for my vegetables. And to top it off, my celery got hit hard by a frost before it was ready for harvesting. I didn't gain anything that year."

But he persevered. In 1936, he was ready to start another season even though his fertilizer bill of the previous year had not been paid in full. Then he ran into a bit of money, and it was off to the races.

"I had borrowed $100 from the Dominion Bank in Chatham in 1935 and by the spring I still owed $25. I decided to go to the bank for another transaction. I hitch-hiked down, as I didn't have enough cash to pay for the gasoline. By the time I got to Woodstock, I was so hungry that I splurged twenty-five cents on a dozen bananas. I ate them all. Funny thing, I'm now allergic to bananas. In Chatham, I borrowed $25 from my brother-in-law and paid off the bank. Then I persuaded the manager to grant me another $100 loan. After all, I had a good credit record. I returned the $25 to my brother-in-law and hitch-hiked back to the Marsh with $75 in my pocket. I figured I was the richest man in the Marsh at that time."

Trucks of John Rupke are loaded in October, 1956, with vegetables for the Hamilton market. Three times a week they delivered to Loblaws and National Grocers.

But it wasn't clear sailing yet. As noted earlier, a frost on June 30 that year killed off all the potato plants.

"I went to the settlement and saw the despair. People were saying: 'We might as well fold up. If there's frost here in the middle of summer, we can't stay.' Of course, the late frost was a freakish thing, and the people began to realize this after the panic had died down."

When news of the loss of potato crop reached the people in the highlands, some of them predictably muttered: "I told you so." There was a definite lack of confidence in the reclaimed area. This was evidenced by the reluctance of township officials to spend money on building firm roads and of local bankers to grant credit. The general feeling was that the area was still a swamp, unsuitable for productive gardening.

In view of this indifference, which lingered for some time, the growers later formed the Holland Marsh Ratepayers' Association. One of its aims was to pressure the municipalities into spending money on much-needed roads. This worked. Later, the group successfully pushed for the paving of the main arteries.

"After the frost," said Walter, "it got terribly hot. In the highlands, everything burned up. But in the Marsh, there was no real problem. The soil was moist. When our lettuce was ready, Dominion Stores grabbed it up. They also bought our other vegetables. We, in turn, bought from other farms and shipped it all to Dominion. Really, that drought was responsible for the changeover from darkness to light."

The farmers in the highlands noticed. So did the township officials and the bankers. There were no more mutters. Maybe those immigrants, the Dutch and all the others, toiling so tena-

Walter Horlings

Celery washing - a view inside one of the processing plants in 1952.

ciously in the dark soil behind the dikes, were onto something worthwhile after all.

Walter and the other Horlings who had moved to the Marsh were convinced they were.

The world war, in which Canada was deeply involved - its soldiers would play a big part in the liberation of Holland in May of 1945 - brought an even bigger demand for the produce. Things started to look up. Accordingly, the brothers increased their holdings in 1941 by seventy acres, buying them at the cheap price of $40 apiece.

In a time when other growers were still fiercely competing for a share of the limited local markets, despite efforts at co-operative selling, the Horlings worked on a system which proved to be a huge success. They pooled their resources and talents, with each one becoming a specialist in his own field. One brother was in charge of production and mechanical equipment, another looked after personnel and the third devoted all his efforts to marketing.

Before long, they began to look beyond the local markets. In 1945, they took in a partner, Abraham Dees, and formed Holland River Gardens. The plant was opened the following year. Now there was no looking back.

Unhappily, rapid growth in the ensuing years brought along an abundance of headaches for the brothers. And the work didn't seem to lessen. Walter, for one, thought more than once of calling it quits.

"We didn't get a big salary. In fact, when the plant was turning over $1 million a year, we got only $2,500 each. We were mainly interested in pumping as much money as possible back into the operation."

In 1959, the business was taken over by Hardee Farms. Walter stepped out, selling his shares while their value was surprisingly high. Others who kept theirs took a beating when the price plunged, particulary one of Walter's brothers who had launched an undertaking in Florida.

"Sometimes I wonder if everything could have been done differently," mused Walter, in his apartment at Holland Christian Homes, a large senior citizens' complex in Brampton where a number of former Marsh growers had taken up abode. "Hardee Farms gave up the business eventually. The building is still there - it houses a number of shops. It is a sad ending, really."

Federal Farms departed also, but other firms moved in. And today the packing industry, consisting of six main concerns, continues to hum along, contributing a large share to the area's economic well-being.

Bradford has benefitted, too, from the extensive support industry required by the agricultural operations.

Mind you, the local seed business is no longer the going concern it once was. Nowadays, with the trend to larger opera-

The enlarged Holland River Gardens plant in 1957.

tions, most of the seed is ordered in bulk from the main seed houses which are located elsewhere. But lots of other things are still being supplied by the local economy, ranging from fertilizers and chemicals to the pallot boxes in which harvested vegetables such as onions and carrots are stored.

Then there are the equipment dealers who supply the growers with tractors and harvesters, the machine shop operators who assist in adapting the machinery for use on the soft soil, the construction people who build storage barns and other structures, and many others who in some way benefit from their close proximity to the marshes.

Some of the smaller growers, commonly referred to as pedlars, sell their crops in much the same way as their forerunners did in the '30's. They deal individually, hoping to get maximum returns. Some take their harvest to the Ontario Food Terminal in Toronto, where it is sold wholesale, and others travel to farmer's markets in nearby cities and even operate roadside stands at their homes. A fortunate few have contracts with stores.

The larger growers deal directly with the packing houses and grocery chains, and some even continue to have their own packing facilities in large barns on the Marsh.

"We're the heart of Canada's vegetable business," Bill de Peuter commented with a hint of civic pride while he was serving a three-year term as mayor of the town. "We're the hub. Mention vegetables and one thinks right away of the Marsh and Bradford."

De Peuter and his parents emigrated in 1954 from Almkerk, a village south of Gorinchem, and landed in the Marsh. They later launched a painting/decorating business.

"Bradford's on the move," he said. "For a long time, there was no real population growth because of limits to our sewage capacity. But this problem has been solved, new subdivisions are being built, and we expect our population of nine thousand to grow rapidly."

Indeed, it did grow, reaching close to fourteen thousand in 1992. The town, named after a borough in England, has gained popularity as a bedroom community for Toronto, within easy commuting distance. Still, it will continue to owe its livelihood to a large extent to the vegetable industry.

As one local writer noted in 1982, on the 125th anniversary of Bradford's incorporation: "When black gold is mentioned, people often think of oil gushing up from the ground. But in the Holland Marsh, that black gold is the soil. It now produces an average of $26-million worth of products at market value each year, provides countless jobs through vegetable growing, cleaning and packing, and has opened the doors to new industry in the area."

~~~

A Great Invasion

The Marsh came of age during the Second World War. The demand for its products grew by leaps and bounds, mainly because of the voracious appetite of the many men and women in uniform and the general shortage of agricultural products generated elsewhere. The growers reaped the benefits.

"We didn't have to sort any more," recalled John van Dyke. "We had no trouble getting rid of even the most malformed carrot."

Despite relatively good times, the Marsh people were still doleful. They constantly agonized over the welfare of their relatives who were struggling under the Nazi yoke. No correspondence was possible. The anguish of not knowing the happenings overseas left little room for joviality.

Residents dug into their pockets for donations to the Red Cross. Auction sales of Marsh vegetables sometimes netted more that $1,000 - a huge sum in those days - also for Red Cross benefit. Moreover, the women spent countless hours knitting hats and gloves for the boys at the front.

In conversations, people displayed real scorn for Hitler's Germany for having spread such a dark curtain over the world. But there were no bitter feelings against those of German background who had settled in the Marsh.

"We certainly didn't blame our German neighbours for the occupation of Holland," said Van Dyke.

The war was eventually won and Holland was freed. In the Marsh, and elsewhere, people smiled again. They tackled their work with renewed vigour.

And the economy purred contently.

The Waterman *arrives in Montreal in 1947. The Dutch ship carried the first contingent of Dutch postwar emigrants.*

Frank Flach, the mailman.

It was in 1945 that Frank Flach moved to the Marsh. Plenty of uncultivated land was still available at an affordable price. But Flach opted for a more expensive tract.

"There was land you could buy for $100 an acre. It was lying in the rough and it had never been ploughed. But I bought land that had already been cultivated and fertilized for a few years. The price was $300 an acre, but this was offset by the fact that we had a good crop right away. If I had bought the cheaper land, I would have lost a whole year just getting it ready."

It took a little adjusting before he felt at home with the spongy soil. Once he learned the ropes, however, he regretted his tardiness in deciding to move down. Even long into retirement, he was still bubbling with praise.

"There are a lot of wonderful things about the Marsh. To cite an example, there is always enough lime in the ground. We don't know why. Look around Montreal - acres and acres of muck, higher than the surrounding areas, and without lime. They had to add it to the soil. Holland Marsh has it naturally. Maybe it's because the Marsh is lower than the area around it."

As a single man of twenty-two, Flach emigrated from Maassluis, near Rotterdam, in April of 1924. He found a job with a farmer at Newton, a village in southern Ontario, and was paid $20 a month plus free room and board. Two years later, he moved to Erieu, near Chatham, and got a construction job. He felt more at home there, especially among the sprinkling of other Dutch immigrants. He soon became acquainted with the Horlings family and began courting one of the girls, Trien. They tied the knot in 1929.

In 1933, after having weathered a few difficult years, often not knowing where the next week's wages would be coming from, Flach struck a goldmine of sorts: he became a rural mailman. For $675 a year - he had to pay all the expenses himself - he took his car on the road six days a week to deposit the mail in the roadside boxes.

"In a time when someone was paid $1 a day for threshing, my pay looked pretty good. The route took about half a day, which left me with lots of time to do other things. Besides that, I was allowed to peddle bread while I delivered the mail. The bread company asked me to take it with me and try to sell it. 'You take along as much as you need. Come back at noon with the leftovers.' I'd sell bread for 7 cents a loaf and pay the company 5 1/2 cents. A penny and a half ... it was worth it for me."

Flach also wholesaled celery, lettuce and carrots sent by train from Bradford by his brother-in-law in the Marsh.

"I would call up on Thursday afternoon and list what I needed for the weekend, and I would have it on Friday. I picked up the crates at the train station at six in the morning and delivered everything to the stores before starting out on the mail route."

Twenty-one years after setting foot in Canada, he quit his mailman job and embarked on a new career in the Marsh. He worked happily until his retirement in 1959.

Soon after the war ended, Canada decided to reopen its doors to agriculturalists from Holland. Across the vast country, many farms were lying fallow for want of manpower. The authorities figured that Europeans experienced in various facets of the farm industry could make a real contribution to the task of giving this important part of the economy a much-needed boost.

The news was welcomed with open arms in Holland, where many people, anxious to make a fresh start after experiencing five difficult and fruitless years of German occupation and seeing little brightness for the future, were knocking on the doors of the emigration societies.

Harvesting was usually a family affair. This photo shows that many hands were involved in the loading of potatoes on Tony Sneep's farm in 1945.

The Netherlands-Canadian Settlement Scheme allowed for the entry of thousands of sponsored agriculturalists and their families. The applicants had to agree to work for their sponsors at least a year. The minimum wage would be $75 a month for married men and $45 for singles. Free housing would be part of the contract.

In the Marsh, the announcement that Holland and Canada had come to terms on an immigration policy was also received warmly. The Verkaik brothers were particularly pleased. With a large acreage, they relied on many hands to look after the crops and the harvest. So they welcomed the new opportunity to hire some people from Holland, ones who knew the job and were willing to work hard to gain a foothold for moving on to bigger things.

"When Jan Rupke went to Holland," said Peter Verkaik, "we asked him to pick half a dozen families for us. We wanted large ones - lots of kids. In that way, we would have lots of workers, and the adult immigrants would benefit from a larger income."

Rupke, still an influential force in the Marsh at that time, was a member of the local immigration committee set up to facilitate the settlement of the new arrivals. Many communities across Canada had formed similar mechanisms. One of Rupke's priorities was to encourage growers, other than the larger ones like the Verkaiks and the Horlings, to make a commitment for sponsoring immigrants.

Verkaik Brothers
VEGETABLE GROWERS - PACKERS - SHIPPERS

BRADFORD - ONTARIO
CANADA
TELEPHONE: 612 SCHOMBERG, ONTARIO

CABLES:
"VERKAIK BROTHERS"
BRADFORD - ONTARIO

His son John recalled: "The thought of having to sponsor entire families - that is, provide them with work and also a roof over their heads - did not sit too well with some people. They loved the idea of having more Dutch people in the neighbourhood, but looking after them was another matter. Dad went around to farmers and said: 'You've got to have somebody.' But the reply usually was: 'How can we? We have no place for them to stay.' Dad then said: 'We owe it to these people. They want to join us, after having survived a terrible war. We've got to help them, in whatever way possible.' Sure enough, he managed to line up sponsors."

A guide for prospective Dutch immigrants, prepared by the Christian Reformed Church, referred to the Marsh in favourable terms. "Our people," it stated, "have made important contributions to the development of this place and the prosperity that has been ushered in over the years." It also mentioned that the produce, mainly potatoes, onions, carrots, lettuce and celery, was being shipped to nearly all regions of Canada, as well as to the U.S., made possible largely by a modern cooling system which mechanically blew ice between the crates stacked in the railway cars.

"An opportunity still exists for Dutch families to establish themselves here," the guide continued, "although at present great difficulties are being experienced in the acquisition of building materials. There is absolutely no opportunity for the settlement of larger groups, but it is possible to put some 100 unmarried men to work. As the settlement is entirely dependent on agriculture, there being no industry, trades people are not in demand."

The *Waterman*, a freighter turned into a troopship, with no facilities for handling women and children, was pressed into service to transport the first big load of postwar immigrants to Canada. More than a thousand people - families, single men and even war brides - said goodbye to their relatives and friends and boarded at Rotterdam on June 17, 1947. And away they went, with only a few dollars in their pockets, but with lots of expectations for a better future.

One of the passengers, Edo Knibbe, didn't let the discomforts and inconveniences bother him during the long voyage. He knew that he would soon see land again - Canada. That mattered most.

Jan Rupke, a cousin of his Dad's, had talked to him in Holland. "We're waiting for young people like you with some know-how." That was all the encouragement he had needed.

With the required farming experience under his belt, Knibbe, twenty-three years old and engaged to be married, ap-

Jan Rupke: "We've got to help them."

plied for emigration. He was assigned a sponsor: the Verkaik brothers. Undoubtedly, he would feel right at home in the Marsh because of his previous work in two reclaimed areas: the Haarlemmermeer and the Noordoostpolder.

"I wanted to get out of Holland badly," he explained. "I couldn't see any future there, no possibility to get started. Why, I had to be twenty-six before I could even be considered for a house or a farm. Mr. Rupke had sold me on the Marsh, and I was fortunate to get a sponsor there, so that's where I headed."

For most of the passengers on the *Waterman*, the voyage wasn't pleasant. There was a complete lack of conveniences; for example, not a deck chair could be found. At night, the men were separated from the women and children. And the relentless swaying and dipping seas resulted in severe bouts of sea-sickness. Despite all the physical discomforts, however, spirits remained reasonably high.

Knibbe became acquainted with many other single men on board. Some were scouts for families nurturing emigration plans and others intended to settle in Canada strictly on their own. A number, like Knibbe, were headed for the Marsh.

On June 26, the *Waterman* docked in Montreal. There were welcoming speeches by officials and other formalities. Then most of the immigrants boarded a dusty and grimy train, which would drop them off at various stops along the route. The ones destined for the Marsh - some counted eighty-one - got out at the train station in Newmarket where their sponsors were waiting with cars and trucks to take them to their new homes.

Army barracks used during the war came in handy. The

Newly-arrived immigrants at the train station in Newmarket await transportation to the Marsh in June, 1947.

New arrivals take time out on a quiet Sunday afternoon for a view of the Marsh from a spot on a hill.

Verkaiks, who wanted big families and got their share, bought a couple of H-shaped huts, 120 feet long, which they cut into sections. These were moved to the Marsh and turned into housing units. On the east side, at Ansnorveldt, single workers stayed in a camp - a two-storey, frame building. The camp mother managed to keep the stomachs full and the beds in tip-top shape.

The newcomers found much of the accommodation in the Marsh a far cry from what they had left behind in Holland. It all seemed so primitive. But they were grateful that they had a place to live, close to their work and among fellow countrymen. Now it was up to them to labour hard, earn a bit of money and eventually branch out to a place of their own.

Another boatload of immigrants arrived in September. Again, a group landed in the Marsh. More came the following year, as the settlement scheme moved into full swing. There were so many Dutch people that some outsiders, not knowing the history, thought the Marsh had been named in their honour.

Ebel Geertsema, who arrived in 1948, once described life in those times: "We worked long days. 'Six days shalt thou labour,' and that is exactly what most of us did. We worked in the fields. Some days we planted, other days we harvested; but mostly we pulled weeds, row after row, on sunny days and sometimes on wet ones too. We wrote our working hours on a slip of paper; always more than fifty per week, for we were in the field by seven and we worked on Saturday until three or four o'clock.

"Saturday was shopping night. All our neighbours could be seen on the main street of Bradford, Schomberg or Newmarket.

No wonder few of us felt there was a need to learn the new language; you could talk Dutch as much as you wanted, and soon even the shopkeepers knew a little Dutch.

"A few of us were homesick. Why do people, already in their middle years, leave their homeland, family and friends and travel to a strange country? Most of us had no time to think

Some of the single men and one of their favourite women - the camp mother.

The newlyweds Edo and Margaret Knibbe and Maarten and Willie Verkuyl.

The wedding party emerges from the little pioneer church.

about such questions. Yet sometimes there were those who were lonely, whose thoughts went back to parents and other loved ones left behind in the old country..."

The immigrants stayed with their sponsors from one to three years. Then they moved on. Some remained in the Marsh, intending to set up their own business. But most left for other areas and other opportunities.

Edo Knibbe decided to stay. He and his friend, Maarten Verkuyl, had come to test the waters, planning to signal their girls if the new country was to their liking. Well, the work wasn't a piece of cake. But they saw the advantages, saved some money, made a few arrangements and advised Margaret and Willie to go ahead with the plan to join them.

Knibbe and Verkuyl were in buoyant spirits as their train sped on towards Halifax in late March of 1948. It felt great to be away from the daily toil and to watch the scenic countryside glide by from comfortably cushioned seats. More importantly, they would soon be reunited with their sweethearts.

"On March 22, our girlfriends arrived in Halifax as war brides," recalled Knibbe. "They really weren't war brides, but that was the only way they could get into Canada. It was stipulated that we had to get married within thirty days. They came with the *Kota Inten*, a troopship loaded with immigrants, some of whom still looked green from seasickness. What a reunion after a separation of nine months!"

Knibbe didn't like the looks of the immigrant train that was about to head for points west. Still fresh in his memory were the disgusting conditions on the one he had boarded in Montreal the previous year.

"After inquiring, we were told there was no objection to us taking the next train. It was like the one we had taken on the way up - clean and comfortable. We didn't want our girls to get wrong impressions of Canada. The trip home was very pleasant, with lots of time for us to get reacquainted."

People in the Marsh opened up their homes to Margaret and Willie. No time was lost in setting the date for a double wedding: April 7, a Wednesday afternoon, at the church in Ansnorveldt. The service would be in Dutch.

"We weren't too fluent yet in English," explained Knibbe. "The minister, Rev. van der Meer, must have translated the entire form. On the day of the wedding, we asked the people we worked for if they would drive us to the church, as we didn't have a car. They did that, and more. They gave us a dinner and then accompanied us to a photographer. When we arrived at the church, we found it filled to overflowing. Chairs were put in the aisle so that everyone could be accommodated. Everyone wanted to see a Dutch double wedding. With all those people, it was impossible for the organist to see who was where, and he actually started playing 'Here comes the bride' three times before the brides made their entrance."

After the ceremony, it was party time. No individual invitations had been issued. In those days, a mere notice in the church bulletin usually brought out the entire congregation for a great time of fellowship, songs and recitations.

"And then we went home. There was no honeymoon for us. It was back to work in the morning."

A happy occasion during the war years: the 1942 marriage in Ansnorveldt of Wilma van der Goot and Stoffer Oosterhuis.

An interesting fact came out after the wedding: Edo and Willie
were cousins whose parents had
been married in a double ceremony
twenty-five years, less one month,
earlier. Not only that, the two were
the first-born in their families, arriving only fourteen days apart.

ADDRESS
DISTRICT SUPERINTENDENT
EASTERN DISTRICT

IN YOUR REPLY REFER TO
B.30091
No.

IMMIGRATION
BRANCH

CANADA
DEPARTMENT
OF
MINES AND RESOURCES

Ottawa, May 2nd, 1947.

Dear Sir:

      With reference to your application for the admission to Canada
of

      Arie Van Der Kooy, his wife, Adriana Van Der Kooy (nee de Ruiter)
and their children, Arie (Jr.), Pieter, Maria Hilla, Sara, Cornelia,
Adrianna and Maartje Van Der Kooy,

presently residing at

      Oostgaag C, 73 Maasland, Holland,

this is to advise that the settlement arrangements for the reception of the
above-named are considered satisfactory and it will be in order for them to
make application in person to the Canadian Vise Officer at the

      Canadian Legation, Sophialaan 1A, The Hague, The Netherlands.

      Provided the proposed immigrants are of good character, in
possession of valid passports, can pass medical examination and otherwise
comply with our requirements, vise for Canada will be granted.

      This letter should be sent to the above-named for presentation
to the Canadian Vise Officer indicated for the purpose of identification.

      Yours very truly,

District Superintendent.

Peter Verkaik, Esq.,
R. R. # 2,
Tottenham, Ontario.

Some Marsh growers sponsored postwar immigrants from the Netherlands.

~~~

An Immigrant's Story

In June, 1949, the Eisen family from Apeldoorn disembarked from the *Volendam* in Halifax and boarded a train headed in the direction of Stratton, in northwestern Ontario, where their sponsor operated a dairy farm. The three immigrants - Johan, twenty-seven, John, fifteen, and their mother, fifty-eight - expected to stay there at least a year, in accordance with the requirements. But just in case things would not work out well on the farm, they had tucked away the address of a friend in Holland Marsh.

This friend, also called John, had landed a job with a German market gardener after an unhappy stint on a fox ranch in Nova Scotia. In his letters to Holland, he had used glowing terms to describe his new environment. In the Marsh, he wrote, there was lots of work, especially in the summer, and there were lots of Dutch people around to make newcomers feel comfortable.

"It did not work out for us in Stratton," related John Eisen. "After two weeks, we were on our way to the Marsh. We arrived at the train station in Newmarket. As John's address was Rural Route No. 2 Newmarket, we surmised that he lived close by. You can imagine our surprise when the station attendant told us the Marsh was at least ten kilometres away."

The Eisens were advised to go to a nearby restaurant where they would be looked after. The owner, a Dutchman, quickly served a meal on the house and phoned Jan Rupke.

"Mr. Rupke, a friendly, elderly gentleman, arrived in about an hour. First, he had a stern talk with my brother, obviously regarding him as the leader of our immigration endeavour. Then he talked to my mother, quickly finding out that she didn't lack any courage. I hardly got any recognition. My mother could stay at Mr. Rupke's house for the time being and my brother and I could board in a camp together with Canadian high school and university students, all seasonal workers hired by farmers in the Marsh."

Rupke was used to being called upon to look after unexpected charges. He took the new arrivals to his car. The suitcases fitted nicely in the trunk. And off they went.

"Our first impressions were great," continued John. "The soil certainly seemed to be fertile, and the flat terrain impressed us, especially since what we had seen of

Mrs. Eisen stands in the doorway of her home - part of a barn - in 1949, shortly after her family's arrival.

Some of John Eisen's campmates take out a few seconds to be recorded for future memories.

Canada so far was mostly hilly country. We had tea and cookies at Mr. Rupke's house while we waited for our friend, John, to show up. He soon arrived, smiling from ear to ear. He took us to the camp - a two-storey structure covered with brick siding - to see the overseer. There was room for us, and we were introduced to many new faces. Two of the leaders in the camp had fought in Holland during the war. And one of the ladies in the kitchen had emigrated from South Africa. We registered, and paid $7 for the first week's room and board."

Four people shared each room in the building, which had been erected behind the public schoolhouse by a number of growers. At first, the thought of sleeping among strangers did not sit too well with John. He had always enjoyed his privacy. But there was no choice, so he moved in. He was advised that any valuables could be left in the office safe. And he was given the address of a physician in Bradford for the required medical examination.

"The forty or so campmates went out of their way that day to help us become part of their way of life. Having always enjoyed a good game of checkers in Holland, I was eager to learn the Canadian game. Another great learning experience was throwing and catching the oblong-shaped Canadian football. I got all the encouragement I could handle, and my first good throw made them jump with joy."

After the excitement of a long and varied day, John had no trouble falling asleep. He was dead to the world. Then a loud bell startled him awake. It was six o'clock.

"We made our way to the big washroom. Water got the sleep our of our eyes. Then we went to the dining room for

John and Johan Eisen have found a comfortable perch for their break.

breakfast. Waiting for us on the long tables were big pitchers with milk, boxes with cornflakes and other cereals, bacon and eggs, sandwiches and more. It all looked like Paradise to me. Most of us, with our ravenous appetites, filled ourselves quickly. And to satisfy our needs for the rest of the day, each was supplied with a brown bag filled with eight sandwiches and a pint bottle of milk."

An army truck, a leftover from the war, brought the workers to the plots owned by Holland River Gardens. John, of course, wasn't aware of the large potholes in the dirt road. When the truck hit a deep one, the milk bottle in his hand fell to the steel-plated floor and shattered into a hundred pieces. To his surprise, one of the boys kindly offered him his, saying he didn't like milk anyway.

The workers were divided into two gangs. Once at the fields, they rushed to the nearest water-filled ditch and deposited their milk bottles in the muddy bottom to keep them cool.

"Then we started our job. We all went on our knees at the beginning of long rows of lettuce plants. We had to thin them out. Those guys worked, and worked hard. In no time, I was way behind. But they all helped me catch up again."

At ten o'clock, it was time for a break. John, as hungry as a bear, quickly downed four sandwiches spread with peanut butter. Then he got a shock: all the boys took off their shirts, revealing sun-baked torsos. Even the boss, George, walked around naked from the belt up. John didn't want to expose his whiteness, so he kept on his heavy, dark-blue overalls. But he had already determined that other attire was called for under the blazing sun.

He had no complaints about the pay. It was forty cents an hour. He normally worked ten hours a day - eight on Saturday - and got Sunday off. When it rained, and work was impossible, there were no earnings either.

"On the Saturday after we arrived, friend John took us on a three-mile stroll to Bradford. It was our first chance to explore the surroundings. I was impressed with it all. I also remember John treating us to an ice cream cone - as much as a cone could hold, for only six cents."

Mother Eisen and her two sons at their home in the Marsh - a section of a barn.

While many newcomers lived in mere sheds, the Eisen family had some good fortune come their way: Johan's boss offered a quarter of his barn. This was gladly accepted. Two walls and a floor were hurriedly constructed. Three weeks after their arrival in the Marsh, mother and sons were together again.

"Camp life had not been that bad," said John. "We had been treated well. On my birthday, at supper time, the female cook came to my table with a big birthday cake with sixteen candles. According to Canadian custom, I had to make a wish and then blow them out. This I did, whereupon everyone sang 'Happy Birthday.' Such a friendly gesture was certainly a treat for an immigrant."

But now they had a home of their own, even though it was only part of a barn without indoor plumbing and other conveniences. To the Eisens, it seemed as if they had taken the first big step on the road to success. Feeling chipper, mother and sons and the owner, a Mr. Morrits, went on a shopping spree for used furniture.

"We bought a beautiful round table with four chairs for $20. We had already bought beds in Stratton, so all we still needed was a stove. Again, Mr. Morrits knew where to get one. My brother and I went for a look. In a back shed, we came across two stoves covered with bird droppings. But at only $10 apiece, they looked like bargains. We picked the best one and loaded it onto the pickup truck. But when our mother saw the old, dirty stove, she refused to allow it inside. All of a sudden, Mr. Morrits explained that he had lots of work to do and quickly left. So we had to face the music alone. But after assuring our mother that the stove would soon be replaced by a more respectable model, she relented and told us to bring it inside. Unfortunately, it lost a leg in transit, which certainly didn't help matters at all."

When November rolled around, most of the fields were bare. The first four months had been busy ones - John often worked until nine in the evening - but now there was nothing left to do. Some of the workers found jobs in surrounding towns. The Eisen brothers, however, remained jobless for most of the winter. With no unemployment insurance benefits, they had to make do with their meagre savings. The temperature dropped and the cold wind swept across the plateau. The inhabitants of the barn couldn't stay comfortable. So they flattened every cardboard box they could lay their hands on and hammered them onto the outside walls to stop the bone-chilling drafts. This worked. But the old Quebec stove still had to do double duty, burning an unending supply of wood and coal.

In January, the Eisens got an opportunity to move out of the barn, and they promptly grabbed it. A three-room house, consisting of a kitchen, a living room and a bedroom, became available. It had no bathroom, no running water and no storm windows. After wind-swept snowstorms, it wasn't unusual to find a layer of fine snow on the kitchen floor.

"For all this, we paid $18 a month," said John. "That was quite a bit. But this stucco house, built on poles, beat the barn by a mile. When we moved, we kept our promise: the old stove

Another day of hard work is drawing to a close.

stayed behind and we bought an oil stove for the new living quarters for $50."

The old stove would continue to heat the barn, now the private domain of friend John. His bed was only a few feet away from it. Still, he couldn't keep warm during the harsh weather, despite sleeping under several blankets and wearing a heavy army coat, two pairs of socks and a fur hat.

"I remember John coming to the door one time, hungry and half frozen. He just wanted to warm up a bit. Out of his pocket came an offering: three frozen eggs."

The arrival of spring ushered in some major changes. First of all, sister Gerda, who had stayed behind in Holland, joined the family in the Marsh.

"There was always room for one more in our house. But her arrival meant that my brother and I had to haul more and more water from our neighbour's tap. There never seemed to be enough. But spring brought more change: we had the chance to become our own boss to some extent. Our neighbour offered us his eight acres or so in a fifty-fifty deal. The owner would not get rent for his land and would not pay for labour either. All other expenses and income were shared evenly."

The Eisens planted thousands of cabbage and cauliflower plants. Although they stood to make little profit that season, they enjoyed working for themselves and gained lots of experience. They also found out that there were enemies about. One morning, they noticed that several plants had been cut off, and immediately suspected the misdeed of a human hand. A more experienced grower commented later: "That's the work of a cutworm. Just dig a bit under the soil and you'll find the culprit." They did - and found it. Without much ado, capital punishment was meted out.

When the cauliflower was ready to be cut, the Eisens found themselves without a tractor and wagon to haul them off the field. To get around this obstacle, they built a stretcher capable of holding four crates. They worked like coolies, but soon buckled under the weight. In the end, they found a kind-hearted friend with a tractor.

Before the introduction of combines, this is how celery was harvested: it was picked by hand, tied in bundles and placed in crates.

With the approach of another winter, the Eisens again looked elsewhere for a job. This time they had more luck, thanks to an acquaintance in Hamilton.

John didn't stay many more years in the Marsh. He had other ambitions. Yet he often has looked back fondly at his early immigration experiences in the muck, realizing that, despite the hardships, these somehow helped to forge a liking for the new land.

He remembered the Sundays, a day off for everyone. After church, many families visited each other or held open house for the singles. Immigration stories were told and retold. People who had settled in the Marsh before the war, often referred to as the old-timers, were particularly in demand when it came to reminiscing. The teens, attired in their finest, went on strolls whenever the weather was nice. They invariably crossed paths in the nearby woods.

With so many single men in the area, girls were in short supply. That's why John was so popular for almost a year after

his sister had rejoined the family. He himself didn't have too much time, or money, to spend on socializing. After all, this was in the days when the meagre earnings went into the family purse and the working boys and girls had to be content with only a bit of pocket money.

Regrettably, learning English was an awkward process for some newcomers, mainly because of the Marsh's isolation and the fact that Dutch was commonly spoken. John picked up a lot of words while working alongside the students in the field. But he didn't feel comfortable with his vocabulary until after he had left the Marsh.

He also observed that the people, in their eagerness to get ahead, sometimes forgot their neighbours. One time, Rev. John van der Meer was fifteen minutes late in arriving for the start of the Sunday morning service because he had to pick up a family whom the others had forgotten. The big growth in the community, with a lot of strange faces coming and going, did erode to some extent the wide brotherhood enjoyed in earlier days.

"But all in all," said John, who now operates The Wooden Shoe Gift and Bible Shop in Renfrew, near Ottawa, "Holland Marsh played a very important part in the history of immigration from Holland. For us, as for many others, living there was a great and unforgettable experience."

Not all ex-Marsh labourers, by the way, are so kind in describing their experiences. In fact, some continue to harbour bitter feelings over the casual way they were treated by their bosses.

One of them, who worked in the Marsh forty years ago, commented: "Whenever I pass through the Marsh over Highway 400, I want to close my eyes so I won't have to look at it. Eight months of my life were spent there, working as a slave for less than decent wages. I once asked for a ride to Newmarket. The answer: 'No.' Why not? 'Because we didn't have a ride to town either when we came to Canada.' A Canadian holiday? 'No, because we are Dutch.' A Dutch holiday? 'No, because we're now Canadians.' Then, as soon as the carrots were out, many workers, particularly the grownup sons of immigrants, were told: 'Out. Help yourselves. We don't have to look after you.' So much for promises."

It didn't take long for newcomers to discover that the arduous life in the Marsh had created harsh, no-nonsense attitudes which placed concern about the success of the crops far ahead of concern about the welfare of workers. The Marsh obviously was not a place for weaklings, for those who wanted to earn a lot of money, for those who expected preferential treatment because they came from the same country as their employers.

Unfortunately, fairness sometimes was totally lost in the mad dash to beat the elements and the market forces.

Mind you, the labourers with grievances were not exactly great models themselves in fostering and promoting good employee-employer relations.

It was a common complaint of the old-timers, the bosses, that postwar immigrants often instigated friction by being pig-headed, conceited and too demanding.

One bitter grower told a Dutch author who was visiting the Marsh in 1950: "They act as if they know best, as if they could give us and the Canadians a few lessons, and as if they have rights to everything. They should have been here during the Depression. Then they would know how easy they have it now."

Although the passage of time has not eroded the acrimonious feelings of some postwar arrivals, we believe that most share John Eisen's appreciation and are proud of having been part of what another Dutch author has described as "a quaint and unique example of our national daring and perseverence."

The West Side

There were anxious moments in the western end of the Marsh in 1946 during the construction of Highway 400, the freeway which cuts through the valley and links Toronto with Barrie and northern resort areas. The south canal was blocked by a temporary dam, resulting in water backing up and threatening to spill over the Town Line - it became Highway 9 in 1965 - and onto the marshland.

Sandbags were hurriedly put in place on the shoulder of the road. But this was hardly a solution to the problem. The blockage had to be cleared - and quickly.

"I decided to call the minister of highways," recalled John Rupke, whose land was menaced. "I didn't know his name, but I remembered it was on my driver's licence. I got hold of him somehow, and asked him for permission to blow up the dam, through which the water couldn't flow fast enough, as the contractor couldn't get his equipment through the mud. I don't remember if he gave permission. I do know that dynamite was used to get that water flowing again."

Highway 400, when finished, did have a positive effect on the Marsh. In a way, it ended the relative isolation, as growers could get to Toronto more quickly and more easily. And the many travellers on the highway, even though they could catch only a glimpse of the black terrain while passing through the valley, usually were left with a lasting impression of a lush and vibrant area.

The highway also put a formal stamp on what heretofore had been a loose entity: the west side. The growers in that area had always felt removed, because of distance, from those in the east end. Now they had a good reason to form a community of their own. Families named Verkaik and Van Dyke were there. Other Dutch names also had appeared on the assessment roll: Winter, Janse, Rupke, Sneep and Noordhof, among others. In 1947, after the arrival of the *Waterman*, even more people moved there.

It was time to give the west side a name. A contest was sponsored by the local Ladies Aid group, Ora Et Labora, which had its beginning in 1943 when a small group of women, members of the church in Ansnorveldt, met informally in the afternoons for some wartime knitting and needle work. The name Springdale, submitted by Mrs. Gerald Rupke, was adopted. She got a book as a prize.

Unlike Ansnorveldt, Springdale is more than a village; the name is popularly applied to the entire area west of the highway. The only cluster is on the Rupke Road - the Christian Reformed Church with its handsome spire, the parsonage, the former grocery store operated for many years by Auke and Addy Ellens, a few large barns and a collection of houses.

In the many years it was open, the store was a favourite stopover for those of Dutch background, as its stock included many goods imported from the Netherlands. But Auke, with retirement in mind, closed the business in 1988. Now a big slice of his attention is focused on his hobby: collecting and restoring

Sandbags hold back the water.

pump organs. He has eight of them, including a model which enticed his wife's father, who loved organs and wouldn't relocate to the New World without one, to make the big jump back in 1928.

By the way, there's still a store in Bradford, Medendorp Delicatessen, which caters to the particular tastes of the Dutch people in the area.

It was in 1948 that the church in Ansnorveldt received a request from a group of its members in Springdale for assistance in acquiring a suitable meeting place for societies such as Ora Et Labora. No place was ever found; the meetings continued to be held in people's homes. There was even a plan at one time to reassemble an old army building, originally acquired for a planned Christian elementary school in Springdale; it had been torn down and moved to a building site.

There was no question, however, that a separate congregation was in the making. The first church service was held on January 2, 1949, in the basement of Harry Verkaik's house, when bad weather and treacherous roads ruled out travel to the

In addition to regular food and household items, the Springdale store of Auke Ellens carried a variety of goods imported from Holland to cater to the particular tastes and needs of the many Dutch people in the area.

east side. From then on, there was no turning back. In August of 1950, it was decided to go ahead with the construction of a church building, thus fulfilling the wish of the people in Springdale and also easing the perpetual overcrowding problem in Ansnorveldt.

Rev. Ralph Wildschut

In the fall, sixteen-foot piles were driven into the ground to support a structure of thirty feet by seventy feet. The actual construction would take place the following year. In the meantime, it was agreed to make the church ten feet wider, thereby increasing the capacity from 180 to 300, and adding a meeting room behind the auditorium. The initial estimate of $4,000 promptly jumped to $11,000.

The builder, Anthony Verkaik, and his assistant, Peter Zwart, laboured through the summer and fall of 1951. The official opening and dedication took place on May 4 the following year. Forty-six families and fourteen singles had requested the transfer of their membership from the church in Ansnorveldt. A few months later, at the organizational service, a simple name was adopted: the Springdale Christian Reformed Church.

Its first minister, Rev. Ralph Wildschut, moved to the Marsh from Falmouth, Michigan, in the summer of 1953. He wrote later: "One thing that stands out in the beginnings and growth of the Springdale church is its diversity. Some of the members were Canadian-born; others had come from Holland many years ago; and still others came from the Netherlands after the Second World War. There was also diversity in the church backgrounds of many members. All this could have created serious problems - and could have resulted in strife. But happily this was not the case."

Over the years, the church has served the residents of Springdale, and beyond, to a degree that greatly strengthened individual faith and sense of community.

The congregation certainly has made its presence felt. In June, 1990, it installed a carillon whose electronic chimes resonate across the often silent fields at noon during the work day, as well as at 8 p.m. on Saturdays and before each church service on Sundays. When the wind blows the right way, people up in the highlands can enjoy the music too.

Plans for a Christian school, put on the back burner in the late 1940's, were reactivated in early 1955. Again, distance and a desire for independence were motivating factors. People in Springdale wondered why their children had to travel all the way to Ansnorveldt to go to school when they could very well put up a building themselves. Besides, the facilities in the east end were swamped.

A school society was organized, a school board was elected and some eighty names were put on a list of potential pupils. The next step was a drive for funds among members of the congregation. This brought in the surprisingly high sum of $14,000. Encouraged, the membership authorized the board to proceed with the erection of a three-room, brick schoolhouse.

On May 2, a site next to Harry Verkaik's house, on the highlands side of the north canal, was picked. This soon became a beehive of activity. Two teachers were hired: Miss Emma Knapper, who would serve as principal, and Miss Arendina Wierenga.

"Alas, September 1 came all too soon, and our school building was not completed, notwithstanding the tireless efforts of the building committee and everyone connected with the construction," said John Rupke, the secretary then. "However, it was with thanks and grateful hearts that we accepted the offer of Jack Israels and Frank Janse to use the spacious basements of their homes as temporary classrooms."

The school was ready for occupancy in late October. It would serve the area well. In 1981, however, its classes ended. The school boards in the Marsh had amalgamated, and the decision was made to accommodate all the pupils in enlarged and updated facilities in Ansnorveldt.

Springdale had lost a vital piece of its community structure. But the reality of economics could not be ignored. Besides, transportation had improved in great measure since the days of parent volunteer drivers and untrustworthy vehicles, in effect narrowing the distance between west and east.

The vacated building, owned by the church, was renovated later for use as a fellowship hall. Members of the congregation,

The completed church stands amoung the black muck.

The Springdale church is taking shape.

Inset: John Rupke

The school was built on the highlands.

Students at the Holland Marsh Christian School in Ansnorveldt in 1955.

and the community as a whole, could rent it for activities such as anniversary parties and wedding receptions. A Spanish-speaking minister even conducted services there for Mexicans employed in the Marsh as seasonal labourers.

"We still think of ourselves as a distinct part of the Marsh," explained one resident. "I guess it will always be that way."

~~~

From the Family Album

In June, 1947, fresh from Oudewater, northeast of Rotterdam, Jacob and Nelly van Hemert and their five children moved into a house owned by their sponsor, Chris Rupke, and became part of the Marsh's growing population.

Harry and John proudly pose with their family's first good car, a 1947 Chevrolet. Its two predecessors are described as "square wrecks," unworthy to be on the road, although they did come in handy many times.

John and Jean

Dad immediately began work on the forty-five acres of fertile, but very weedy, muck land. His earnings of $75 a month barely covered the cost of the basic necessities, even though the house was rent-free and the family members could eat as much lettuce and carrots as they wanted. Precious dollars were expended on groceries, clothes and footwear, as well as for education at the Christian school and worship and fellowship at the church.

But, like most other immigrants who had arrived in Canada virtually penniless, the Van Hemerts made do with their meagre resources and struggled on.

Dad worked hard. There was no other way. He experimented with growing *witlof*, also known as Belgian endive. And he was a firm promoter of starting lettuce and celery in the greenhouse in February and setting the plants outside in the begin-

The day's task of this gang is to remove the many weeds growing among the onions.

ning of April, which meant a three-week headstart on the seeded vegetables. In 1950, he became foreman for Peter Verkaik, who had a larger acreage.

Son John joined the farm's workforce right after his graduation from the Christian school. At age fourteen, he was a swamper, responsible for loading trucks and railway cars. He soon got a better job; he was put in charge of all the farm machinery.

"At age fifteen," he recalled, "I was on the truck without a licence, delivering produce to the plant and railroad cars in Bradford. I sputtered a bit, saying: 'What if the OPP (the Ontario Provincial Police) stop me?' Mr. Verkaik said: 'Then you send them to me.' In those days, the police were not so strict and the farmers enjoyed a bit of extra respect in the community."

It was in the fields where John met his future wife, Jean ten Hage, also a member of an immigrant family. "Would you believe," he chuckled, "that already at five in the morning, the starting time for cutting lettuce, we would sneak a hug behind a huge pile of lettuce crates?" Now and then Jean would come to the house to help his mother, who by then had four more children to look after.

In 1955, John became foreman in charge of some 30 workers, all immigrants from various parts of the Netherlands. He also was on the road a lot, making deals with buyers from the big markets. The produce then was being shipped to such places as the West Indies, Newfoundland and Montreal. For extra excitement, Verkaik bought more land outside the Marsh, and John had to help with the removal of trees and the ploughing of the peat soil.

The following year, he was involved in a farm accident that changed the course of his life.

"The fingers on my left hand went through a sprocket and a chain on the onion combine. It happened in the middle of harvest. I was hospitalized for a week in the worst time and in the best time - the worst time because the crop had to come off before the frost, and the best because the Lord took hold of me to send me back to school."

Mother sets to the task of wiping the traces of a dust storm off her furniture.

Sara, Audrey, Alex, Irene and Nelly check up on their rabbits after church. Peter Verkaik's storage barns are seen in the background.

Nelly, Irene and Sara van Hemert check out the size of the sunflower growing in their backyard.

The girls of the Ten Hage and Keen families are busily at work in the lettuce patch.

These scenes are part of the carrot harvest.

Three dozen head of lettuce are packed into each crate for shipment to the Kroger grocery chain in Cincinnati, Ohio.

John left the Marsh in 1957 to attend a Christian high school in Grand Rapids, Michigan. He continued on to higher education, and was ordained as minister in the Christian Reformed Church, in Edson, Alberta, in 1965.

He and his wife return to the Marsh every year to visit with family and friends and to look around the areas they used to know so well.

Then there is their photo album, chock-full with pleasant memories....

An eight-row seeder is employed on an onion field.

The onions are combined and left on the field for curing.

The lettuce workers take a break from their arduous chores.

The farm work wasn't exclusively devoted to vegetables. There were even Christmas trees to look after. First the seedlings were planted. And in a few years, the trees were big enough to be cut and taken to the market.

John fills the tank at the Supertest pumps. The building in the background is used for the storage of onions.

It's early spring in 1954, and a start is made in the greenhouse on three crops: lettuce, tomatoes and flowers.

John van Hemert, the future minister, is about to leave the Marsh with another load of vegetables.

Greenhouse tomatoes are ready for the Toronto market.

~~~

And the Swamp Flourished

Disaster Strikes

The growing season in 1954 started out the same as in the previous years. There was the usual time of preparing the soil, followed by seeding and weeding and harvesting the summer crops. People grumbled about it being too hot or too cold or too wet or too dry. And there were the trite complaints about prices being too low.

Then autumn arrived. The ritual continued: young and old pitched in to get the late crops off the fields before the freezeup. The old-type onion toppers rattled from morning until night.

That fall, however, was noticeably different from other years. Rain fell frequently, hampering work in the fields. Wagons sank hopelessly in the soggy ground. The going was slow.

Then, for almost six days straight, it rained incessantly. By now, the Marsh was saturated and large puddles formed in low-lying areas. The pumps worked overtime. Even so, more water accumulated.

Many among the three thousand people in the Marsh began to show concern. Some kept an anxious eye on the swollen canal and noted its level was creeping even higher due to the tremendous runoff from the highlands. They began to wonder if the dike was sturdy and high enough to hold back all that water.

The thought of being hit by a flood never preoccupied the Marsh inhabitants. Sure, they knew that they lived below the water line in the canal and that many of the early dwellings were built on poles, a ways above the ground level, as a precautionary measure. Some were acutely aware of occasions when water seeped through weak spots in the dike. But there seemed to be a general feeling of security, a faith in the ability of the drainage and pumping works to handle any problems.

The calm before the storm.

No one gave much thought to the idea that the Holland River would try to reclaim the Marsh for its floodplain.

Some of the Dutch residents had a brief encounter with dreadful thoughts in 1953 when they heard the shocking news reports from Holland. A combination of a vicious gale and a high tide had resulted in the breaching of dikes and the inundating of a large area of the country's southwestern parts. The water would claim nearly two thousand lives.

"We live behind a dike too," the thought went. "If a big storm hits, we could be under water. People could drown. The land could be destroyed."

A rescue party looks for signs of stranded people.

A woman and her dogs are ferried to higher ground.

But there was no unpredictable sea beyond the dike. There were only hills, as dry as bone, and below them a canal for diverting water, including the North Branch of the Holland River, away from the Marsh.

The unease quickly disappeared. But it trickled back, and even spread, in the fall of the following year when the puddles didn't want to go away.

Then came Friday, October 15.

The weatherman had ominous news: a hurricane which had been sweeping northward from Haiti, roaring across the eastern United States and wreaking great damage, was heading for Ontario. Tropical storms rarely reached that far. But this killer would - and it had lots of punch left.

As noted earlier, it rained cats and dogs for days. But this downpour was nothing compared with what Hurricane Hazel was to unleash on the Toronto area, including the Marsh, on

that black Friday. By late afternoon, some gauges had recorded a rainfall of more than seven inches. And more was to come, as the storm's eye was still approaching.

The Holland River within the Marsh began to overflow its banks. The drainage ditches also spilled over. Unable to drain away - the pumps were useless at this point - water blanketed large areas. The puddles had grown into small lakes.

Auke Ellens was unusually busy in his little grocery store in Springdale. Customers bought extra supplies of milk and bread, just in case they should get stranded for a few days. Then they hurried home and kept their ears glued to the radio for the latest reports on the storm's progress.

Edo Knibbe had other things on his mind. He was poking around in a wrecking yard, hoping to find spare parts for his truck.

"I was so worried about getting that thing in order again that I really didn't notice the downpour that much. Only when I got home did I realize that we could be in for some problems before the storm was over."

But Knibbe, who lived in the southeastern section of the west side, had no idea of the seriousness of the events taking place at the north canal.

Water roared, then thundered, from the highlands via two components of the Holland River - the Schomberg Branch to the west and the North Branch. The canal just could not handle all this flow, and water began pouring over the dike into the Marsh below.

Knibbe recalled: "John Rupke, who seemed to be everywhere, phoned me at 7:30: 'That water is going over the dike fast. You better get out quickly.' I didn't hear anything except the sound of rain, and I could hardly believe what I was told. My first thought was to get some men together and lay sandbags. But then I decided to heed the warning. I put the kids and a couple of suitcases on the truck. My wife Margaret and I quickly moved some of our belongings upstairs, although I really did not think that the water would ever get high enough to flood the floor of our house. And then we set out for higher ground."

For a few minutes, the rain stopped, and the sky was clear. The stillness was eerie, scary. Then it started again: the wind, the rain, the darkness.

"Nothing seemed to go the way it was supposed to," said Knibbe. "The roads were full of gullies. It was raining so hard that I couldn't see the wooden bridge across the canal. So I got out of the truck to check with a long stick whether it was still there. It was, and we drove safely across it. We followed the Town Line (now Highway 9) eastward. A three-foot wide creek east of Highway 400 had turned into a raging river, boiling two feet high over the small bridge. About ten cars were standing there, the drivers debating whether it was safe to go across."

It didn't take long for Knibbe to make up his mind. He turned around and went back to the wooden canal bridge, again checked to see if it was still there, then followed the south canal bank road and, after much manoeuvring, ended up on Highway 400.

The intention was to reach the place of Knibbe's cousin in Toronto. But the family never came close.

"While going south on the 400, we encountered a huge landslide near the Town Line. The whole side of the hill had slid down, all but blocking the southbound lanes. A Gray Coach bus was lying on its side in the median. That was enough. We turned off at the Aurora sideroad and sought refuge at the farmhouse of George and Helen Sportel."

This couple - they would later move to the Marsh - had already taken in thirty people. But no one was refused shelter. The men were bedded down on the lower floor, without blankets, pillows and beds, while the women and children spent the night in the bedroom quarters upstairs.

Sleep was out of the question for Knibbe. At 11 p.m., with a break in the weather, he ventured outside, intending to check up on his house. It had been on his mind constantly.

Somehow, he got there. And, much to his relief, everything seemed intact. But the fields were under water, as was part of his driveway. He carried some of his furniture upstairs, all the while still not thinking that the water would ever reach the ground floor, still two feet up.

"The road was dry, and I followed it north for about four hundred feet past our house. Then it disappeared under water. All was fairly quiet, but I was worried about what was happening to all those north of us who were in lower-lying areas. Did they get out? Was the water still rising? Nobody knew what was going on except in his own immediate surroundings."

Sensing the destruction to come, Rupke piled his wife and seven children into the family car and set out for a motel on Highway 27, one of the routes to Toronto.

"When we got to the top of a

The Springdale church and parsonage under water. At the height of the flood, the truck was completely submerged.

Onlookers stand on the dike near Peter Verkaik's house as rescuers set out.

Nellie Verkaik, outwardly calm but a bundle of nerves inside, gathered together her seven children, including a baby of six months, and got them ready for quick departure.

"Our main concern," she recalled, "was to get to higher ground to avoid being stranded. We thought of the baby and the food that would be needed."

Verkaik pulled his house trailer, normally used for holiday trips, onto the dike. Then he went back to get his family. They made it safely across a bridge, which was still intact, and stopped at the home of Peter's brother, Harry, which stood on higher ground overlooking the canal and the Marsh.

More and more people arrived there. Before long, about seventy souls were crammed inside, occupying every available spot. Candles provided the only light. There was no clean water.

"Everyone kept calm," said Mrs. Verkaik. "But I don't think anyone slept, other than the little ones. I remember seeing my husband staring out the window towards our place. I knew what was going through his mind. I couldn't help but think: 'The Lord gives and the Lord takes away, but in the end He'll make everything all right again'."

hill near Woodbridge, we could see the road through the valley ahead of us had water rushing across it. A tow truck heading in our direction was hauling a car through it. When its driver drew level with us, he called out that this was to be his last trip for the night because conditions were so bad. With traffic piling up behind me, I was trying to make up my mind as to whether to chance going through that water. Suddenly, a car shot past us, got about forty feet across, then slipped to the side of the road and went over the guardrails, ending up in what was probably only a little creek, now swollen into a river."

The impatient driver never escaped from the torrent. His body was recovered later. Shaken over this incident, Rupke turned his car around and headed for Highway 400 which would lead him to his sister's home in Toronto. He finally arrived there at 3 a.m.

Peter Verkaik had been at the International Plowing Match near the village of Breslau, a two-hour drive west of the Marsh. It had been a miserable day there too, with rain and mud galore.

His headlights cut a swath through the rain and the darkness as he drove over the dike to his house near the north canal on the Springdale side. A ways ahead of him, he noticed water rushing across a dip in the road, falling like a waterfall onto the marshland.

"By the time I got to the house, I realized we were in for something terrible. Water seemed to be everywhere. There was no doubt in my mind that we were in for a major flood. I said: 'Mom, we've got to get out of here'."

The fury of Hurricane Hazel caused rivers and streams in the Toronto area to flood in a manner never known before. Raging torrents of foaming water ripped out bridges, upended cars, tore houses from their foundations and swept all before them, as nature went completely out of control.

In the Marsh, the situation grew progressively worse. The water gushing down from the highlands ate away obstinately at the inner side of the north dike. Then the worst fears came true: a section of the dike, where the North Branch entered the canal, was washed away under the pressure. The water streamed unhindered onto the lowlands.

Art van Dyke, a native of Oud-Beijerland, south of Rotterdam, a resident of Canada since 1927 and of the Marsh since 1942, walked around his house, eyeing the water with apprehension. He kept reassuring himself that it wouldn't reach the foundation. But this hope faded when it crept higher and completely surrounded the house.

Still, he decided not to leave the Marsh. He and his family, and a number of flood refugees, would stay on the second floor, out of reach of the water.

"I told everyone that as soon as the water got up to the floor joists, we would move the furniture upstairs. Well, we did end up moving the furniture, and we even managed to roll up the broadloom and get it upstairs too before the water had a chance to ruin it. All through the night, I sat on the stairs and watched the water creep higher and higher. It ended up at least three feet deep on the ground floor."

Addy Ellens remembers: "Everyone who stayed in the Marsh believed that, at its deepest, the water would come only to floor level or a little above it in most houses. Therefore, they moved what they could to the second floor and took their cars up to the dike. Little did they realized what the next few hours would bring."

She was single then, living with her parents, Cornelius and Nellie Radder, on the Springdale side. Her husband-to-be, Auke, had recently purchased the grocery store built there in 1953 by her brother, Cor.

Auke and Addy closed the store at 8 p.m. and, with the help of neighbour John Weening, placed most of the stock on the top shelves.

"We went to the home of my parents and helped carry some things upstairs," recalled Mrs. Ellens. "I remember my father opening a trapdoor leading under the house so that the water could come in. He said that if we tried to keep it closed, we would make the house into a boat. Then followed long hours of wind and rain."

The police closed the highway for the passing traffic.

John de Peuter and his family inspect the house in which they sailed during the storm.

Residents survey the situation from the roadside.

Some people in Bradford, told of what was developing in the Marsh, drove down the treacherous canal road towards Springdale, intending to pitch in with sandbagging or whatever other help was required.

"It was no use — sandbagging was never attempted," one of them explained. "We wouldn't have been able to stop the water from coming over the road. We could hear people out in the Marsh calling for help, but it was so dark we just couldn't do a thing."

At about eleven o'clock, according to Mrs. Ellens, the rain abated and the wind stilled.

"Dad called Auke, my brother Leon and me outside on the front porch. We could hear the water streaming over the dike. The stars were out. Dad said: 'We're now in the eye of the hurricane. Later, the wind will rise from the opposite direction and the rain will fall as heavily as before.' He was so right. After that brief respite, the storm returned with its former savagery. No one could sleep. The great flood in Holland the year before was still fresh in my mind. I had read how people secured themselves to the chimney, and I thought: 'How can we survive out on the roof when the water chases us out there?' My mother read to us from the Bible."

The Radders and Auke went upstairs when the water continued to rise. Huddled in the darkness, they listened to the screaming wind and the pouring rain and heard the sickening sound of the water doing its damage.

Radder had placed an old pump organ on chairs in the living room. The sound of it falling off signalled to the people upstairs just how high the water was getting. The windows broke and some of the family's possessions floated away.

At 2 a.m., there was a strange sight.

"Out the back window," recalled Mrs. Ellens, "we saw, as it were, a ghost ship, a house, approaching, riding on the waves.

It was clearly visible because it was so near and all so white. It hit the barn and swerved and crashed into a small greenhouse, caught on something and whirled around, and then passed between our house and Bill Winter's and stopped down the road, tangled in hydro wires. This was the home of the Bassie family. We found out the next day that it was empty, but at the time we were worried about the family."

When the water rose, John de Peuter nailed the door of his rented frame house shut and plugged all the cracks he could find with rags.

"We hoped someone would come and pick us up. But when the dike broke - no chance."

Father, mother, their twelve children and a neighbour's son who had been playing at the house moved to the upper floor. Then something unusual happened: the rushing water and the powerful wind tore the house off its posts and it began to float away with its astonished occupants.

All over the Marsh, the homes, barns, implements and cars sat abandoned in the water.

Only a short distance away from the road, piles of bags with onions lay in the water-covered fields.

"I had this old car sitting out in the yard, a Frontenac," recalled son Bill, "and I yelled to my father: 'Hey, Dad, my car's floating away!' But it was us who were floating away."

The family spent the remainder of the dreadful night huddled about various parts of the floor, trying to keep the drifting house in balance as it spun about in the pitch blackness. It bumped into houses, barns, greenhouses and hydro poles, jarring those inside with a sickening thud each time. But no one panicked.

De Peuter, besides barking orders to the children to run to one side or the other, calmed everyone down by saying it was a good house that floated like a boat and they could always hang onto something if the worst happened.

The rocking was so violent that five-year-old Bastian became seasick.

Finally, a fence at Highway 400 ended the wanderings. A white flag made from a bedsheet was flown from a window to attract attention. Rescuers spotted it and promptly took the seafarers to the Bradford town hall which had been turned into an emergency shelter.

In 1953, when disaster struck Holland, the De Peuters lived near the Biesbosch delta. The water reached their backyard. When they moved to Canada the following year, to land above sea level, they never imagined that they would soon experience another flood.

The family's incredible adventure would be the subject of conversation for years. When talking about Hurricane Hazel, people would ask: "Did you hear about the De Peuters?"

Besides the Bassie and the De Peuter homes, five other dwellings were dislodged by Hazel and set adrift upon the waves. One, abandoned earlier by the Oostveen family, ended up a short distance away from the De Peuter one at Highway 400. Another one held the Postma family, but they fled into the attic, cut a hole in the roof with a saw and were later rescued.

The house occupied by Cor Krygsma and his family stayed in place, but an adventure ensued nevertheless. Everyone fled upstairs, away from the rising water, and into a floorless, windowless attic. There, in the pitch darkness, they perched

When the water receded, a monumental task awaited the flooded-out residents.

on the ceiling joists, and spent an uncomfortable, scary night, unable to attract anyone's attention. Finally, Krygsma managed to make a small hole through which he could wave his hand, and rescuers came in the morning to ferry the family to safety.

Then there was Arend Hanemaayer, who had decided to bed down and hope for the best. He awoke during the night, stuck his hand from the bed and found six inches of water covering his floor. He wasted no time in moving everyone upstairs. A boat docked at the second-floor window at daybreak. The family clambered in, and soon they were on dry land again.

Although the Springdale side was hit the hardest, because of the breach of the dike there and the fact that Highway 400 prevented much of the water from spreading away quickly, the entire reclaimed area was under water. At the height of the flood, water spilled over the highway and into the larger section of the Marsh. More passed through a culvert under the highway - a part of the old Holland River - which necessitated an effort by some frantic growers the next day to plug it with trash, much to the dismay of those on the other side.

Still, whether one had to put up with six feet of water or two feet, the flood was a terrible disaster for everyone who lived or worked in the Marsh.

Near Ansnorveldt, Eise Beimold had decided to ignore a warning to move to higher ground.

"I figured that it couldn't be all that bad and decided to stay. So did John Miedema. We just didn't want to abandon our property; it was part of us. At two o'clock in the morning, with water everywhere, a call came from the police: move or we'll come and get you. With no choice, we moved out in a truck."

They, too, ended up at the town hall. Some of the people there, exhausted and emotionally drained, tried to bed down. But none slept. Before the break of dawn, many headed back to the Marsh to ascertain the state of affairs and the extent of damage.

~~~

The Big Cleanup

At six o'clock in the morning, Edo Knibbe climbed a high hill and beheld a beautiful lake.

"Everything seemed so quiet. It appeared as if nothing was wrong. But then I spotted roofs of houses sticking out of the water, and the reality of what had happened really began to sink in."

Rescuers in motorboats had been crisscrossing the inundated Marsh, searching for stranded people, since the first glimmer of light. They found quite a few.

A boat also stopped at the house of Cornelius Radder.

"Part of our house had a flat roof, and this served as a dock," explained daughter Addy. "We left our place with only the clothes we were wearing and my knitting. As we went past Auke's store, we saw the broken windows and could imagine the mess inside. His truck, parked near the church, was completely under water. What sad sights met us all along that unforgettable ride."

At the dike, the Radder family disembarked. Others who had been rescued earlier stared silently at the water, undoubtedly thinking: "This is the end. Everything is gone. We'll have to start from scratch somewhere else." Later, other boats took everyone to Highway 400, where cars were waiting to complete the transit to Bradford.

During the night, the population of Bradford had doubled. Most of the Marsh people had left for higher ground when the water came. Residents of the area rose to the emergency magnificently, opening their doors to friends and strangers alike. Hundreds were also accommodated in the town hall, which had been converted into a refugee centre, staffed by Lions Club members and volunteer women.

During the days that followed, these compassionate people would spend countless hours preparing free meals for the homeless and packing sandwiches and filling coffee jugs for the men manning the pumps and repairing the dike.

While the rescuers continued their task - even the army lent a hand with amphibious vehicles - a group of mainly Dutch growers was summoned to a meeting in Bradford by George Horlings, who had been given the monumental task of getting everything back in order. This burly man wasted no time. He was determined, despite the initial defeatism shown by many, to get rid of all that water, and clean things up, make repairs and get crops in the ground in spring.

"George handed out the jobs," said Peter Verkaik, one of those called. "Everyone got something to do. My brother Jake, for instance, was put in charge of cleaning up all the junk. George dispatched the men right away with the words: 'Get busy. Time is of the essence.' Finally, I was the only one left. I thought I was getting off easy; I had not been given a specific job yet. But George turned to me and said: 'Pete, I have a little task for you: you're going to pump that Marsh dry'."

Verkaik, known for his business acumen, and his ability not to mince words, jumped into action. His first priority was to get pumps. As there was no natural drain out of the Marsh, the only way to get rid of the water was to pump it back into the canal from which it had come so brutally.

"A reporter from the *Toronto Star* was there, and a few of

George Horlings

us, including a lawyer, got into his car. The lawyer had an idea: let's go to Coulson's Hill, a high point on Highway 11, and use the radio in the reporter's car to get hold of an army general in Ottawa and tell him to get all the pumps at his command shipped to the Marsh right away. We made contact with Ottawa, finally got hold of someone in the army and were told: 'Sorry, we don't have those pumps'."

This initial setback didn't deter Verkaik, who would become known as Peter Pump and his brother Jake as Jake Junk. He told Ontario Hydro, the provincial power utility, that he needed engineers for expert advice, and four of them were on the scene the next day. He also contacted a mining company, and soon three large pumps and ancillary equipment arrived, the forerunners of what would become an impressive display of pumping power.

The pumps were placed at the northeastern point of the Marsh, where the canal emptied into the continuation of the Holland River. Temporary power lines were installed. And finally the big moment arrived - the pumps were turned on. But nothing happened.

"A bit perplexed, we phoned the mining company. What do we do now? It turned out that the spouts had to be pointing in the air - not turned downward, as we had them - in order for the pumps to work."

Seventy thousand gallons of water per minute were being pumped out initially. As more pumps were brought to the scene - at one time, twenty-five were operating - the flow increased to 200,000 gallons per minute. Manned by willing workers, the operation ran night and day.

"A lot of people offered help," said Verkaik. "One farmer came with a number of little gear pumps which, of course, were useless. Still, we appreciated the offer. Tragedy does bring out the best in people."

He had little rest during those days, which he later would describe as the most difficult in his life. His family, living in a motel room, hardly saw him. If he wasn't on the ground, supervising the pumping operation, he was in the air, in a helicopter, surveying the progress being made in getting the Marsh dry again.

"Most of the time," recalled his wife, Nellie, "I had no idea where he was. But I knew that he was all right. He wanted that land dry as soon as possible so that everybody could get back to their homes and their fields and fix things up for another season. And I knew that nothing would stand in his way to bringing that about."

She fed herself and the children a mash called *hutspot*, as carrots and potatoes were plentiful in the area. Little else was available, though, and the menu turned out to be the same every day. One day, in a moment of exasperation, she told herself that she would never eat another carrot in her life.

Verkaik decided to install another pump at the North Branch to speed up the drainage in that area. He was able to acquire a good diesel-operated one from Leamington, a ways beyond Chatham.

Peter Verkaik, at right, discusses the pumping operation with a government official.

This augur-type pump was among the many employed to drain the Marsh.

"When it got here, the water was receding already. But we figured it was a shame to send it back, so it was installed. Later, when the accountants came around to check out all the borrowed and donated inventory, they asked: 'Peter, what about that pump over there? Do we take it out?' I said: 'No, it stays. Just write it down as part of the flood relief.' You know, that pump is still there today."

The draining of the Marsh was completed in little less than a month. The *Bradford Witness*, a local weekly, reported on November 17: "The large pumps which have been operating almost without letup for nearly four weeks have finally ceased operations. The Holland Marsh is now entirely cleared of water, both east and west of Highway 400, with the exception of a few pools lying here and there in land depressions. The task of the pumps and their operators was a tremendous one, but it is a job well done in shorter time than at first thought possible. The big job of mopping up debris and getting the irrigation ditches cleaned out still remains to be done. But with continued fine weather, which favoured the pumping operations, the Marsh gardeners are hopeful, indeed optimistic, that this can be accomplished and a crop produced the next year."

Some experts had estimated that the draining would take two months, and possibly longer. But most of the growers, while still shaking off the shock of the disaster, had touted different ideas. George Horlings, the hard-driving chairman of the cleanup efforts, had told a reporter: "We want to get on that land again. And as soon as possible."

John Rupke recalled: "There was a comment by an engineer on the day after Hazel that the Marsh might not even be completely drained that fall and that there would be no crops the following year. Well, we didn't like that comment. And we proved the fellow wrong."

In the days immediately following the hurricane, there was deep concern over the possibility that some people might have drowned. With the Marsh residents now scattered over a large area, in temporary shelter, it was difficult to determine if everyone had eventually made it to safety. There were sighs of relief when the news media reported that apparently no one had found a watery grave.

It turned out to be a much different story in the immediate area of Toronto. The death toll there reached eighty-one.

The damage inflicted on the Marsh was great. Houses were ruined. Personal belongings were spoiled beyond repair. The onions which had been drying in the fields were gone. Many of these onions, along with potatoes, wagon platforms, fuel tanks, boxes, crates and anything that would float, amassed on and along Highway 400 and an area stretching up to two hundred feet west of it.

The water even had lifted up the 1 1/2-foot-deep layer of topsoil of a six-acre potato field and carried it toward the highway. There it settled atop a field of carrots. It would take an array of dumptrucks all winter to put everything back in place.

When Edo Knibbe was able to make it back to his place, just newly built, he found the water lapping against the windows. The furniture that he hadn't been able to move upstairs was under water and deemed a total loss.

Any mail? It's worth a check.

"Three weeks later, I found that everything didn't fit. The water had expanded it all. Windows didn't rise. Doors didn't close properly. And when the wood dried, matters grew worse. The glue let go, and everything fell apart. Moreover, the drywall was worthless and the insulation was useless. Many painstaking hours of labour were required in later months to put everything back where it had been."

Peter Verkaik: "We had two hundred gallons of fuel oil stored in our basement for the furnace. Someone had left the top off the tank, so all the oil got out, floated on top of the floodwater and soaked into everything, including the wood. We smelled oil for years after that."

John van Dyke: "What a mess. The drainage river was filled in places with large cakes of soil and a variety of garbage. The fields were littered with all kinds of crates, bushels, boxes, drums, bags of onions, hotbed sash. Anything not too heavy had been tossed from one place to another. Here and there one could spot an outhouse, of which there were a good many in those days. I had the good fortune of finding a wooden keg on my land. I thought it might contain some of the fruit of the vine. Unfortunately, the plug had come out as it rode the waves and the water of Hazel mixed with the precious moonshine."

As Auke Ellens was cleaning up his grocery store, he found a get-well card stuck to the window of the meat cooler, with the inscription: "Cheer up, the worst is over." But he found it difficult to smile. He was forced to dispose of his entire stock in case some of it might be contaminated.

The nearby Springdale church also was badly damaged; it sagged on its foundations. The pews were grotesquely warped, and the small pipe organ and other items such as hymn books were a total loss. During the restoration, and the con-struction of an addition consisting of parish hall, consistory room, furnace room, washroom and library, the congregation would hold services in other churches in the area. The building would be useable again in the spring of 1955, and at the rededication in May, sincere thanks would be expressed to all the people who had helped out during and after the flood. A marker on the exterior front wall of the church denotes the maximum height of the floodwater.

All roads leading out of the Marsh were guarded twenty-four hours a day to prevent unauthorized transports of produce from leaving. The vegetables that had been in contact with water were deemed unfit for sale and had to be destroyed. And this was being strictly enforced, not only for safety's sake, but to protect the high respect which the Marsh people had been able to win for the quality of their products.

"The men on guard duty were chosen mostly from among the Marsh growers and were sworn in as temporary police," said Van Dyke. "They took their job quite seriously. They would stop anybody, even their neighbour and next of kin, show their badge and exercise their authority to the limit."

Jake Verkaik, in charge of salvage operations, felt it necessary to issue a statement to clarify the proceedings: "Holland Marsh vegetables have not been condemned by the Department of Health. But the movement, sale or offering for sale of any produce which had been submerged in floodwater is forbidden. This order will be rigidly enforced by the Ontario Provincial Police. There are quantities of Holland Marsh vegetables in dry

Arie van der Kooij, a grower on the east side, checks out the depth of the water.

A lone wooden shoe among the debris.

*The mess inside the store of Auke Ellens; inset,
the merchandise neatly displayed after the cleanup.*

storage and in packing houses. These, of course, have not been touched by the floodwater and may be shipped in the customary manner subject to government inspection."

Art van Dyke returned to his home as soon as the water level was below the floor boards.

"The first thing we did was get heat in the building. It was the heat that let us save so much of our house."

But many other families did not make it home so soon. Their places had to be fixed up first. Some stayed with relatives or friends. Others camped in trailers set up on the hillside near Harry Verkaik's home, the shelter for so many during that awful night. About seventy families - no fewer than 350 men, women and children - lived in a big trailer camp set up by the Rotary Club at the town park. That's where they spent the winter.

Soon after this camp opened, the *Bradford Witness* reported: "A visit to the camp reveals the entire assemblage of trailers and huts laid out in orderly rows. An oil stove serves each trailer or hut for heating and a propane gas stove for cooking, while each unit is lighted with electricity."

Ten-gallon oil drums served as garbage containers. Sanitation facilities were provided in a new cement-block building, divided into sections for men and women. Each part contained four toilets and three showers, and there was a room for the washing of clothes as well. A Red Cross emergency hospital was located in a forty-foot trailer. Another building, created by joining together two huts supplied by Ontario Hydro, was used for storing food and personal belongings, such as baby car-

Mrs. Nellie Radder and daughter Addy were amoung those who lived in temporary shelter at a trailer park in Bradford which would not be disassembled until the spring.

riages, for which there was no room in the trailers.

"A large recreation building or play centre had been erected by putting three hydro huts end to end," reported the *Witness*. "This should help to ease the tension during the day by providing play quarters for the children of families temporarily living in crowded circumstances."

Jake Verkaik.

Debris left by the flood covered the shoulders of Highway 400.

When news of the flood was spread by the media, many people from nearby communities drove toward the Marsh for a look. But only officials could get right on the scene.

Outside of the people directly or indirectly affected by Hazel's wrath, perhaps no one felt the blow harder than relatives and others in the Netherlands. They knew what it was all about. The major flood of the previous year was still in the forefront of many thoughts and conversations.

The Rotary Club of Harlingen forwarded a letter to the club in Bradford: "We would like you to know that we, in the homeland of so many of your fellow countrymen, are greatly shocked by this bad news and we sympathize with all in their distress. Since the liberation by your heroic army, we feel that a common bond exists between our countries and we therefore follow the happenings in your country with particular attention."

The Dutch minister of agriculture, S.N. Mansholt, visited the Marsh for a first-hand look at the havoc. Dutch government officials stationed in Canada did likewise. Even Queen Juliana, who had become head of the House of Orange upon her mother's abdication in 1948, sent a message to the stricken area: "Deeply grieved because of the serious disaster suffered by the Dutch immigrants on the Holland Marsh, we send our sympathy to those affected by the storm."

But there was more than messages. Actual money began to

flow in from near and far, including Holland. A relief fund was set up and the provincial government promised matching financial help. Any building that had moved more than two feet from its foundation was considered a total loss and the owner was eligible to receive a payment of $5,000. Enough money would

The water is receding, and soon the occupants of this house can start cleaning up. The high water level is clearly visible on the outside wall.

become available to look after the restoration of homes and fields and the replacement of furniture and equipment. Most people also had private insurance coverage. Still, even though some residents would later boast that they actually benefitted from the flood, in a material way, there were others whose losses were not totally covered by the across-the-board payments. And no money could replace, say, the family photo album or other personal effects which some people, in their haste or the excitement, had forgotten to place high and dry.

Clothing depots were set up. Private firms sent mechanics into the area to help the farmers repair machinery which had been under water. Mennonites from the Kitchener area, to the west, moved in by the busload, tackling the roughest of jobs without uttering a word or asking for remuneration. Yes, many people cared.

In late December, two men looking for Christmas trees came across a frozen body submerged in a swampy area. It was that of John Nagy, forty-one years old and a native of Hungary, who had been unaccounted for since the storm.

At the time of the flood, grave fears were expressed for his safety. His house in the west end, in which he lived alone, was under water. Neighbours kept an anxious eye on the work gang at the dike, expecting him to show up there. When the water was being pumped away and his body was not found, it was thought he might have escaped the flood and gone elsewhere. Alas, it turned out that he had plunged into the rising water at the spot where a wooden bridge had washed away.

The news of the grim discovery shocked many. Hazel had claimed a life in Holland Marsh after all.

When the weather allowed, crews and individuals were busily employed in digging out miles upon miles of drainage ditches, repairing roads and bridges and fixing up houses, barns, driveways and so on.

As part of the cleanup, the canal was dredged. The soggy silt was dumped on the far side of the dike, sometimes flowing like lava against houses, garages and storage sheds. This caused unending complaints. But officials had a ready excuse: the work had to be completed before the spring thaw and runoff and no time could be wasted in arranging other methods.

When the time rolled around for the growers to work the soil and seed the crops, the anger had subsided. Fears that little would grow for the first two or three years proved to be unfounded. As usual, the plants flourished and the harvest was abundant.

In the end, the disaster resulted in little long-term damage. In fact, some growers claimed that the thorough soaking improved the fertility of the muck and, for a year or two, got rid of certain pests.

Jack van Luyk explained to a reporter: "What the flood did was clear the land of a lot of old fertilizer and junk. It actually did the Marsh good." Another resident commented later: "If it weren't for all the houses, we should flood the Marsh every year. The soil thrives on water."

~~~

Glimpses

A scene from the past: a few decades ago, onions were pulled out by hand and placed in rows for drying. Then they were loaded in bushels and brought to a tractor-driven topper. After the tops were removed, the onions were graded and bagged and set out in the field for curing.

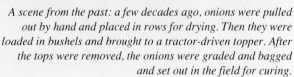

In 1947, the year he landed in Holland Marsh, Arie van der Kooij grew witlof, commonly referred to as Belgian andive, in his garden. He was quite pleased with the results, which provided the family with many pleasant meals. Witlof grows in the darkness - and there is plenty of that in the Marsh soil. Another favourite vegetable of the immigrants from Holland was boerenkool, known here as kale, which makes up a tasty, and hefty, meal when mashed with potatoes.

Mud is a perennial problem in the Marsh. Heavy equipment has a tendency to sink in the organic soil, especially after a rainfall, so much of it had to be adapted to handle the conditions. The tractors of Peter Verkaik, employed in pulling a mired transport truck to freedom, provide an example. The other photo shows a car hopelessly stuck in a sea of mud near Highway 400.

The year is 1967. It's been very wet, and the growers are worried. They've called in W.A. Stewart, the minister of agriculture, who is third from right, and other officials. Yes, the community spirit, so evident during the difficult days after Hazel, never seems to wane. When there was a problem to be overcome, the growers banded together and presented a common cause for action. They never failed to help each other out of difficult situations. For example, in the fall of 1958, George Keep, owner of a ten-acre garden, came down with a bad case of pnemonia. His wife was in a quandary; how could she get the crop off the field before it rotted or got destroyed by frost? She didn't have to worry for long, however. An army of volunteers showed up to look after the harvest. She would be in the same predicament in 1961 when Keep contracted tuberculosis and spent eight months in a sanatorium. Again, a large group of acquaintances and friends would come over to get the potatoes out of the ground and look after other chores.

The Marsh has been called the Salad Bowl of Ontario. Its crisp lettuce is in great demand. This harvest photo was taken in 1969.

In the introduction to this book, mention is made of the unveiling of a plaque in Ansnorveldt which recognizes the significant contribution of the Dutch to the Marsh's development and growth. Similar plaques - one in Dutch, one in English - were unveiled later at the town hall of Nieuwe Pekela, in Groningen, where the Horlings family used to live. The mayor, Tale Evenhuis, who had been at the ceremony in Ansnorveldt, did the honours. A number of people from Canada were on hand, including one of the Horlings - Mrs. Frank Flach. "It was just a big coincidence," recalled her husband, a former grower in the Marsh. "Trien and I were travelling in Holland and heard about the planned unveiling. The mayor asked us to attend. And we were glad we did - it was a big affair."

In the summer of 1974, a small group of retired men got together to discuss a common concern: there wasn't much for them to do in their somewhat isolated surroundings. They agreed that organized activities were needed for the elderly to fill their leisure time, which they had plenty of now that the younger generation had taken over. In November of that year, the Holland Marsh Senior Citizens' Club was formed. The parish hall of the church in Ansnorveldt was used for the meetings, first bi-weekly on Thursday afternoons and later weekly. This was only a temporary arrangement; the members wanted a structure of their own. Accordingly, a building fund was launched. Donations from the seniors grew to $8,000. Applications were also made for government grants. Meanwhile, showing a typical grab-the-horse-by-the-collar attitude, the men decided to go ahead with the construction themselves on the site of the old public schoolhouse. With the help of a few tradesmen, they succeeded in getting the roof on before the start of the winter in 1976. Another $9,000 was raised in the next few months through a canvass in the neighbourhood and an auction sale. Grant money also began to trickle in. The building fund eventually totalled $43,700, enabling the centre to be completed. The building doubles as a community hall. "We believed a community facility like this was much needed here," John van Dyke, the club's secretary, said at the official opening in October, 1977. "Well, we have it now."

Just when everything seemed to be going great in the Marsh, disaster struck again. On May 31, 1985, the sky darkened ominously. The wind began to howl. Many people, rightfully alarmed, scurried for shelter. Suddenly, a churning funnel cloud swept across the open terrain, tearing buildings to shreds, uprooting trees like matchsticks and tossing cars and trucks about like toys. Sixty storage buildings were sucked right off their foundations and destroyed. The tornado's swath of destruction extended to nearly every property in the valley. When the storm died down, the residents could only stare with bewilderment and incredulity at the damage. Fortunately, there was no loss of human life within the diked area. With exemplary resolve, the people tackled the rebuilding. One, whose barn had been flattened, commented: "I sometimes get the feeling that I've experienced it all - a hurricane, a flood, a tornado, frost, hail, drought. You name it, we've had it. But that doesn't mean that we're now free of bad things. Everything goes in cycles, you know. I have a feeling that, someday, Hazel will return...."

The Trapper

It was early November. A sprinkling of snow covered the ground and a raw wind swept across the virtually barren fields. It was a good day for staying indoors. Indeed, many of the growers had decided to do just that, and perhaps even go on a shopping trip to town, considering it was Saturday and little pressing work was left now that another season was rapidly drawing to an end.

Not Peter Brouwer. Bundled up, insulated from the bone-chilling dampness, he walked a few steps from his house to the south canal and lowered himself into a small motorboat. The temperature at water level seemed doubly cold. Undaunted, he started the motor and negotiated his craft along the surprisingly smooth water, carefully hugging one of the banks.

He had embarked on a regular check of his trapline, which covered some twelve miles of canal and river. Hopefully he would return home later in the day with a few fur-bearing animals such as beaver, mink and muskrat.

The earnings wouldn't be that great. But any extra cash would come in handy, especially since a big chunk of the land he co-owned with his older brother had been rented out, due to illness, and he had been forced to dig into savings to pay the bills that mercilessly kept on coming.

Brouwer was a tyke of six years when his family, including father Kees, mother Helena and brother Chris, moved to the Marsh in 1936, two years after the first group of settlers had arrived there. His father had acquired a five-acre farm on Juliana Road, north of the settlement.

The decision to move to the Marsh from the Chatham area had been an easy one. The senior Brouwer and his wife had worked in the sugarbeets after emigrating from Krabbendijke, in the province of Zeeland, in 1926. It was hardly the golden future that they had dreamed about. Then the Depression came along, which made matters even worse, especially after the crops were in and there was no other work around to tide the family over until the arrival of another spring. Brouwer refused to go on relief, so he scraped by, earning a few pennies here, a few dimes there, and searching nearby fields for white beans that had escaped the harvest.

This painting shows a beaver family hard at work.

Kees Brouwer takes a break from his field work.

John Siervogel, a friend who had moved to Bradford, informed him about the Marsh. He visited him in 1935, inspected the land, talked with a number of other people, and immediately grabbed at the chance to become his own boss.

For $50, he bought two construction shacks which had been used by workmen during the building of a bridge across the river on Highway 11. These he assembled into a dwelling on his newly-acquired land. It consisted of two small bedrooms and a kitchen which had to double as living room. Tarpaper covered the roof and the sides. There were no inside walls, and no insulation of any kind, which made the living conditions almost unbearable during the frigid blasts of winter.

"One morning," recalled son Peter, "the temperature was forty below Fahrenheit outside, according to the thermometer, and, believe it or not, it was twenty below inside. The kettle on the stove was frozen solid. You see, our little shack wasn't heated at night. We couldn't afford coal, and nobody wanted to stay up to put wood on the fire. In the morning, we stayed under the blankets until the kitchen was warmed up and mother signalled that it was okay to come out. We closed the bedroom door behind us, so the warmth wouldn't escape from the kitchen, and we snuggled up to the stove as closely as we dared. One time my brother got too close - and burned his behind."

The cry of anguish must have been in Dutch, for that was still the predominant language used in the household.

"I was born in Canada," explained Peter, "but I learned Dutch before I learned English. I don't even know when I start-

ed to use English. My mother is still alive — she's eighty-nine now — and I talk to her every morning over the phone in Dutch. I'm told that I don't even have an accent."

Despite such a background and an obvious interest in things that are Dutch - some telltale miniature wooden shoes grace his living room - he has never visited the Netherlands.

"I don't want to go either. I'm not a traveller. I went to Florida once and got homesick. They couldn't get me into an airplane if they paid me. I'm quite content to stay right here."

Father Brouwer grew lettuce the first year. There had been consternation and doubt when a late frost hit. But new crops were quickly planted, and they flourished. In the end, Brouwer didn't do too badly, considering he had no previous experience in vegetable growing. The harvested lettuce was placed at the end of Juliana Road where a truck belonging to Church Transport of Bradford picked it up for delivery to a commission house in Toronto.

The entire family pitched in during the field work. The two young boys did mostly weeding. There was no such thing as summer holidays for them, nor for any of the other kids in the area.

For Peter, as for most of the others, the work in the muck would become a way of life. He and his brother eventually teamed up with their father. When Dad died in a pickup truck mishap, the sons carried on the operation in partnership, growing leek, celery, squash and a variety of other vegetables on some thirty acres. Peter's wife, Florence, a former city girl from Toronto, proved to be an invaluable worker. Chris, by the way, has remained a bachelor.

"I have always made a living from the Marsh," said Peter. "I've never had to borrow money. I always earned it first and then spent it, rather than the other way around. I don't have

Before the arrival of machinery, onions were graded by hand by the Brouwer family.

much, but I am satisfied. In that respect, the Marsh has been good to me."

Notwithstanding such sentiments, he hesitates to recommend muck farming to anyone. Sure, the quality of the vegetables is second to none in North America, and there is money to be made if the price is right. But the many uncertainties, year after year, can exact a toll.

"Who wants a job that relies on Mother Nature? Look at this year. We had a poor summer — lots of rain — and the onions didn't mature. Hundreds of acres are no good. And now the soil is so wet some growers are not even going to get their carrots out. When I see all that hard work, all those long hours, go to waste, I am glad that my sons got an education. One is a regional policeman and the other a civil engineer."

Brouwer, thoroughly chilled, but humming with contentment, returned from his check of the trapline with three beavers, half a dozen muskrats and even a raccoon that had the misfortune of being trapped. It was an average catch. Now, in the warmth of his basement, he began the painstaking chore of removing the pelts.

"I'm not an expert in this," he said, gingerly slicing through the tissue. "It takes me about three quarters of an hour to skin a large beaver. One has to be very careful not to damage anything. The slightest imperfection will bring down the price. Even so, I don't make much money doing this. Maybe a couple of dollars an hour when you calculate all the time I put into it. It's a diversion. I enjoy doing it."

And it's necessary too. The drainage commission and the individual landowners don't like beavers cutting down trees,

Another scene from the past: washing potatoes in tubs.

building dams and hindering the flow of water in the canal.

Brouwer's been trapping since he was fourteen. Too young to get a licence then, he simply got one in his brother's name. It was common to spot a string of pelts drying on the clothesline. For twenty-five years, he paddled a canoe to his traps. It never tipped over. He would have been in difficulty if it had, as he doesn't know how to swim. The canoe now occupies an honoured spot in his basement.

"Many years ago," he said, "there were twenty-two trappers here. Now I am the only one. It's because there is no great demand for fur anymore. The animal activists can be blamed for that. The prices also are not what they used to be."

He produced a 1990 transaction statement from the fur auction which showed that the prices of the eighteen beaver pelts he marketed that year ranged from $42.55 to $8.05, depending on size and condition. One muskrat pelt sold for fifty-seven cents. But a mink brought in $95.

"Last week I got a beaver that was fifty-one pounds. That was a big one. So I looked up some statistics in a book and found out that the biggest one on record is 112 pounds. I've got quite a ways to go yet to reach that. You know, it was the beaver that built up Canada. Our country wouldn't exist as it is now if it hadn't been for the fur trade. This trade is one of the main reasons the Dutch came to North America in the 1600's in the first place. I guess I'm carrying on a tradition."

Peter Brouwer is shown in 1955 with a bushel filled with muskrats.

The animals are skinned.

The pelts are dried and then brought to the fur auction.

~~~

Behind the Scenes

"It's a real League of Nations here. Over there, to your left, lives a Chinese fellow. Next to him is a German. That place over there has been sold to a Dutchman..."

Art Janse was taking us on a grand tour of the Marsh, his home turf since he was six. He knew the area as well as anyone else; he'd been on the municipal payroll as drainage superintendent since 1979, and was a member of West Gwillimbury Township council, with responsibility for drainage, for eight years before that.

"That's the old Holland River," he said, pointing to a marshy expanse on the far side of the canal, on the Springdale side. "It was dammed off when they built the dike. Did you know that sixty-four thousand acres drain into the Marsh? That's quite an area. You can imagine all the water that ended up here during Hurricane Hazel."

He turned his van onto Rupke Road and stopped at where a concrete ramp dipped into a waterway - the old river within the Marsh. A dozen yards away, flanked by clumps of reed, was one of two barges used for keeping the river clean of silt and weeds and thus ensuring an unobstructed flow.

"It was built in 1976 by Louis Devald, a Hungarian on the Marsh. The paddlewheel type was his own design. This machine replaced dragline buckets which for various reasons were deemed unsatisfactory. Later, we built another barge of the auger type at a cost of $160,000. Now we have one for either side of the highway. There are three ramps for sliding them into the river."

Devald, who has worked on the Marsh since he was eleven, is a self-taught mechanical wizard. With the help of his son-in-law, Alex Makarenko, he has earned a solid reputation as a manufacturer of custom-built harvesters, planters and other farm machinery for anyone who comes knocking on the door.

Back on the road, Janse spotted something else he thought worth noting.

"See those yellow barns over there? That fellow is Lebanese. No, they're not all Dutch around here. We have all nationalities."

The van turned back onto the dike.

"Under normal conditions, the water in the canal is about four to five feet higher than the land below the dike. Of course, when the Marsh was reclaimed, the gap was much narrower. That's because the soil has shrunk so much over the years. It's getting lower all the time and someday in the distant future we'll be down to clay in many spots. It's too bad, really."

Janse slowed down at the two pumphouses on the west side which are looked after by Ted van der Goot and his wife Grace.

We had been there a few weeks earlier, when the rain came down incessantly for days, saturating the land and causing pools of water to form in low-lying spots. Many people were worried

This is one of the three ramps used for lowering the Marsh's dredges into the river.

There is a barge on each side of the highway.

then. They had seen the same thing happening prior to the arrival of Hurricane Hazel.

During the latest wet period, Van der Goot kept a steady watch on the level of the drainage waterway - the continuation of the North Branch within the Marsh - which flowed next to his fourteen-acre farm. He and Grace were responsible for activating the pumps, located a few steps from their house, whenever the water reached a certain height. The municipality paid them by the hour.

"Well, we are keeping those pumps going twenty-four hours a day," explained Van der Goot, who took over his father's operation in 1959. "We are getting rid of a lot of water.

Some people are saying that all this rain is reminding them of Hurricane Hazel. Let's keep our fingers crossed that we don't get a break in the dike this time."

There was no break. Still, all that water had caused a few hairs to turn grey. Harvesting machinery sat idle in the mud, unable to be used in getting the matured vegetables off to market. A volunteer brigade of high school students from Woodbridge, an area community, and others, waded through the quagmire to aid growers in salvaging as much as possible by hand, but in some areas rot had already made inroads.

This was - and is - an inescapable part of life for the Marsh people.

Janse, who was born in the Chatham area where his father, Frank, had settled in the 1920's after emigrating from Walcheren, in the southwest of the Netherlands, offered a few words about Van der Goot's domain: "An auxiliary pumping plant with two pumps was put in at this spot in the early 1950's. That was after Highway 400 cut the Marsh into two sections. The main pumping station was on the other side, at the northern end near Highway 11. After Hurricane Hazel, another pump was added here at the North Branch."

He stopped his vehicle at the gates controlling the flow of the river east of the highway. He got out with a hammer in hand and opened one of the gates a bit, allowing water to back up into the west side.

"It's getting a little low here, so we'll let some water in. The level has to be checked constantly. This keeps us on our toes."

A trace of snow covered the bare fields. But is was far from pure white, the result of strong winds sweeping along arid patches of muck.

"Dust storms can be a problem here. I've seen entire ditches filled in. High winds cause erosion, especially if the surface is on the dry side and the crops are not fully grown yet or are off the fields."

Why don't the growers plant trees as windbreaks? The centre of the Marsh is conspicuously devoid of tall growth.

"Trees harbour bugs. And they would cut into the amount of useable land. The best thing is to keep the soil on the wet side. You see more and more sprinkler irrigation systems in operation during the dry spells. That's a spectacular sight."

Not all fields can be irrigated, however. So, in order to effectively protect their crops from wind damage, many growers seed barley in their carrot and onion fields and grow the crops on raised beds or hills just like potatoes.

Janse next pointed to a problem which directly affected him, as the drainage superintendent, and the members of the overseeing drainage commission.

"The dikes are not too strong in spots. In fact, sections sink now and then and we have to raise them up at considerable cost. We're having constant problems with part of the north dike, which is built on peat. It wasn't put on a solid base when it was constructed. It's made of whatever came out of the canal at that time."

Nevertheless, the barrier, elevated two feet after the hurricane, is sturdy enough to withstand any onslaught. Well, not quite.

"If we get another Hazel, the water will still come over the dike no matter what we do. There's such a large area that drains

Art Janse

Van der Goot checks the grate at this pumphouse for debris.

The organic soil tends to dry out quickly during dry spells, so sprinkler systems are used to keep as many fields as possible moist.

into here. The flood of '54 was a freak occurrence: all the wet weather, the saturation and then the hurricane with its tremendous downpour. We may never see that again, although when it rained and rained this year and water stood in the fields, unable to drain away, some people did get a bit concerned. They remembered."

The van rambled along a muddy road. Janse had more things to show.

A private pumphouse installed by growers.

Dike repairs are under way.

"At one time, there were six hundred drainage ditches in the Marsh, just about all them dug by hand by the early settlers. Now there are hardly any left, except for the ones alongside the roads. Most of the fields have been tiled. See that dip in the

One of the few ditches that remain.

road over there? That's an old creek bed from the original marsh. The house there is flooded every spring because it's so low. With all the rain this year, you could really spot the old creek beds."

He turned onto a dirt portion of the south dike, closed to general traffic. A tract of dense bush was on the left. The absence of muck at that point undoubtedly was the reason for this land being undeveloped.

"This is how the dike looked in the early years. Some ruts in the dirt. Lots of trees. Really wild. I remember helping my Dad clear his land when we came to the Marsh after the war. We chopped a lot of wood in those days."

He stepped from the van to inspect open spots in the thin layer of ice that covered the canal.

"Looks as if a deer dashed across. There are a few of them around. You know, we had a grand time at the canal when we were kids. We used to go fishing a lot - for pike, catfish and carp. Some kids even went swimming. And in the winter, if the conditions were right, we skated for hours."

A ways ahead, in a clearing, stood a house. Its owner, who used the dike for access, was stacking firewood in anticipation of a long, cold winter. Janse stopped for a brief chat, then turned his van around and retraced his tracks through the snow.

"We're having a bit of trouble with this part of the canal. A few fast-moving streams are silting it in. You can see it there. A lot of trees are falling in too. I'll have to get a dragline to clean it out. There should be no obstructions."

He drove north through Ansnorveldt and stopped at the main pumphouse. Two pumps there were being looked after by a full-time employee under his supervision. There was also a machine which removed duckweed and other debris before the water reached the intakes.

"Look there, behind the grate. Those are the original intakes, now long out of use. See how high they are above the water level? That shows you how much the soil has dropped since the days of Professor Day. The inlets we have now are getting to the same stage; they are about four inches under water and one of these days they'll run dry. One of the pumps already sucks air and vibrates if we try to run it. That's why I've recommended to the drainage commission that a new pumping station be constructed."

The pumphouse at the North Branch.

The water drawn to the main pumphouse is covered with duckweed and debris.

In 1992, the commission finally embarked on a $1.4 million project to update the pumping facilities. Contracts were awarded for the construction of a new pumphouse five hundred feet from the old one, with four pumps worth $75,000 apiece capable of draining 65,000 imperial gallons per minute. The operation is to be computerized and totally automated.

The van was back on the canal road. Janse carefully negotiated a curve. Only a few feet of earth separated the pavement from the water. This lip used to be a lot wider before the canal was dredged in the post-hurricane cleanup.

One of the huge pumps is lifted out of the pumphouse for repairs.

"A few cars have gone off the road, and a few people have drowned. See those pipes in the water? They're for irrigation. There are enough pipes going through the dike to flood the Marsh with two inches of water in twenty-four hours. See that little shack we just passed, by the roadside? A fellow used to live in it. Tarpaper shacks were common around here in the early days. What you see today is Paradise compared with what it used to be. There are some beautiful homes. Notice how some have been built at dike level just in case we have another flood."

Janse parked at his house on the west side, a stone's throw from the canal. The trip had ended. It was time for him to check his greenhouses, a business he had carried on for more than three decades.

"I grew tomatoes for a long time, and then I went into English cucumbers. Now there are flowers. It gives me a bit of extra income. I really didn't want to carry on my Dad's business. I just couldn't see myself spending any more time on my knees in the mud."

This is the main pumphouse. Contracts were awarded in 1992 for a new, up-to-date facility.

~~~

It's Going, Going...

A sign stuck in the ground near the roadside at the Muck Research Station had a clear-cut message: "ORGANIC SOILS DISAPPEAR. Main reason: decomposition (oxidation). Rate: 2.5 cm per annum."

Next to it was a post about five feet high with markers showing the rate of soil subsidence every ten years. The top of the post denoted the level of the marshland in 1930.

This little display gave visitors to the station, and particularly the landowners in the Marsh, the grim news that at the present rate of decline, of one foot per decade, not a great many years are left before large areas of the irreplaceable natural resource will be down to clay. Unless, of course, steps are taken to slow this process.

One effective way is to control the water table. Its height, according to experts, should be raised when the crops are off. And during the growing season, it should be lowered gradually to between sixty and ninety centimetres below the soil surface, depending on the crops. Such measures would diminish oxidation.

A ten-year study at the station concluded that a water-control program could reduce the annual rate of subsidence from 2 1/2 centimetres to .47 cm. Already some of the growers have banded together to lay pipes from the canal to tile drains in their fields, thus ensuring a ready and steady water supply.

"Many experts have been saying that the Marsh as we know it has about fifty years of life left," explained Matthew Valk, who was senior muck crops specialist and the person in charge at the station until his recent retirement. "However, we have determined that with the proper management, including overhead sprinkler irrigation, the lifespan can be extended. The number of years will vary from area to area, depending on the depth of the remaining organic soil. I estimate it to be anywhere from fifty to two hundred years."

It's an inescapable fact that one day the muck will be gone and the bed of clay and silt will be supporting other types of farming. Organic soils do break down and decompose when they're cultivated and used for agriculture. Other destructive factors are also at work: the dust storms when there's not enough rainfall, compacting by machinery and humans, and even the occasional fire.

Still, most of the Marsh has considerable life left. That's why the handful of personnel at the research station, which became part of the government-run Horticultural Research Institute of Ontario in 1969, are continuing with their efforts to assist growers with crop problems and finding ways of preventing specific difficulties from arising.

This includes the testing of hundreds of breeding lines for their adaptability to the climate and soil of the Bradford area, chemical and non-chemical control of insects and diseases, and physical and chemical methods of weed control. Moreover, advice is offered on crop management such as nutrition, spacing, cultivation, dates of planting, precision seeding, and so on. Growers can also get guidance on soil management, including control of the water table and erosion prevention, and on proper handling of vegetables after harvest.

Farmers can call in daily on an Agriphone for the latest information on, say, spraying for onion maggots or carrot rust fly.

The present research station was built in 1971.

Matt Valk shows post which indicates the rate of subsidence of Marsh soil. The top denotes the level in 1930.

help with certain crop production problems. A temporary building, called the Horticultural Experiment Station for Organic Soils, was erected the following year, and Professor C.C. Filman was put in charge. The present structure, simply called the Muck Research Station, dates back to 1971.

Matt Valk, who hails from Rotterdam, was one of fifteen graduates of an agricultural school in Dordrecht who headed for Canada on the *Waterman* in June, 1947. Twenty years old, single, and with a background in agriculture - both his grandfather and father were in the greenhouse vegetable business - he figured the time was ripe for emigration. He had no trouble securing a sponsor, the Prins family on Bernhard Road.

"When I saw the Marsh, I knew right away that I would feel at home," he recalled. "I was familiar with the type of soil and, having seen some of the other landscape, realized that this was a unique area. I stayed. Some of my classmates who had grown up with clay soil had other feelings. And when they found out that weeding was done by hand and that a big part of the day was spent on one's knees, they left."

But after two summers, he quit the Marsh too. He had heard favourable stories about the vast wheatfields of the West, the legendary Prairies, and that Dutchmen had gone there. Perhaps, he thought, there was an opportunity

Or they can drop over to glance at specific test results.

The test plots used for trying out new varieties and other experiments are an important part of the operation. Graduate students of the agricultural college at the University of Guelph, the old stomping grounds of Professor Day, look after many of them sedulously.

The station, just off Highway 400, had its beginnings in 1947 when a group of Marsh growers approached the agricultural college for

This was the first station, where growers could get advice for overcoming crop production problems.

even better than the one offered by the Marsh. In 1949, he travelled to Saskatchewan on a scouting mission.

"The people I stayed with were very friendly. In fact, I had the impression that they regarded me as their son. After all these years since then, we still correspond. But I didn't feel at home in the West; everything was so much different from what I was used to. So I headed back to Ontario."

Determined to build on the education acquired in Holland, he enrolled at the agricultural college in Guelph. Three years later, he was the proud owner of more credits: degrees in horticulture and agriculture.

During his student days, Valk had been back in the Marsh quite often. In the summer, when there were no courses to attend, he had been a labourer at the research station. The black soil, it seemed, had gotten into his blood. So it was no surprise to friends when he decided not to pursue a possible career as a university lecturer and instead joined the work force of Holland River Gardens in 1954. He held the position of production manager, in charge of the eastern operations, until 1965. Then he went to England to work for a company that produced and marketed onions. Four years later, he was back in the Marsh, this time as a muck crop specialist at the station, responsible for advising growers on a myriad of things.

He had obviously found his niche. His heart had been close to the station ever since his studies. It was there, in the early 1950's, that he met his future wife, Jane, an entomologist engaged in research at the time.

Valk was put

Edo Knibbe displays celery grown in test plots.

Agricultural students at work at the research station.

in charge of the station in 1973, holding the dual job of co-ordinating research and carrying out advisory work.

He was assisted for a long period by fellow Dutchman Edo Knibbe, also a 1947 arrival, who joined the station staff in 1974 after operating his own fourteen-acre garden in Springdale and serving a stint as farm manager for Holland River Gardens. In his new job, Knibbe was in charge of the field operations and all the technical work.

"The biggest problem facing the growers today," explained Valk, "concerns the availability of crop protection materials. Few of them are approved - and few are coming down the pipeline. Really, the cost of developing pesticides for small crops is too high. Besides, there are stricter regulations to contend with."

The next biggest problem, he continued, involves marketing. "Production efficiency is running ahead of consumption.

In his student days at the station, Valk felt comfortable in his Dutch footwear, even inside.

We are making such big strides in combatting diseases and pests and other problems that the yields are high and of good quality. But there are not enough markets. The growers are looking at more exports - in fact, one third of the carrot crop already goes to the U.S. But other countries are doing the same."

Even in retirement, Valk continues to benefit from his deserved reputation as one of the best experts around when it comes to matters dealing with muck farming. He's an independent consultant, working out of a van equipped with a cellular telephone, a video camera and a weather radio. Growers can hire him at an hourly fee to advise on correcting and preventing problems and on ways to gain maximum results.

Valk was succeeded at the station by Mary Ruth McDonald whose title, research scientist, is indicative of the continued emphasis being placed on the study of such vital matters as conventional and biological methods of insect and disease control. She is a specialist in plant pathology, with experience in the Marsh as a pest management scout and later as a pest management adviser with the ministry of agriculture. She is completing a doctorate degree on the biology and control of cavity spot of carrot.

But no amount of pest and disease control can forestall the eventual disappearance of the highly valued topsoil and the lucrative industry it supports.

With such a bleak future facing the muck farmers of a few generations down the road, it is surprising that there is not more open discussion on the subject. Few people seem particularly perturbed. Obviously, the growers prefer to focus their thoughts on the current state of affairs in their industry and leave events beyond their lifetime as matters of conjecture.

Even so, there is no shortage of private opinions on the use that might be found for the diked area once the muck is gone. Some growers believe the Marsh will be turned into a giant

Matt Valk: "In 1948, I bought my first car, a 1927 Chevrolet, for $150. I had a lot of fun with it, going to Muskoka and other vacationing spots on weekends. At that time, I was making sixty cents an hour and working fifty-five to sixty hours a week."

landfill site to handle the ever-mounting volume of garbage generated by the millions of residents of the Toronto area. Others are convinced that it will be reflooded in response to demands by city folk for more recreation space.

The prevailing view, however, is that the Marsh will continue to function as an agricultural area.

~~~

Epilogue

"Holland Marsh is the richest vegetable-growing land in Ontario," intoned a commentator for a slide presentation produced by the Ontario Ministry of Agriculture. "Just one acre of this organic soil yields sixty thousand pounds of perfectly-formed carrots, or a thousand crates of celery, or forty-five thousand pounds of onions, or twenty-five thousand heads of lettuce. The Marsh grows millions of dollars worth of vegetables a year...."

Yes, it has come a long way since the days when John van Dyke sweated for three weeks in his lettuce patch on his allotment behind the settlement, cutting a few crates each day. In the often unendurable heat of summer, thirty per cent of his plants had shot up into seed.

"When you look back," he commented, "you begin to realize that the Marsh is really a marvellous piece of growth."

Most of the first growers could ill afford mechanical equipment, so the work in their fields was done by hand. Later, an enterprising Chinese immigrant who owned a horse made his services available for a fee. Then home-made tractors, as well as factory-made ones, came on the scene. The evolution is continuing.

At harvest time, large, sophisticated pieces of machinery move up and down the fields. They're like little factories, with

The Marsh carrot harvest in full swing.

workers boxing or bagging the lush produce as soon as it's out of the ground.

"How times have changed," remarked John Rupke's wife, Katherine. "I can remember seeing John and his brother in the ditch, working a pump by hand to irrigate the celery."

Mechanization and chemical weed control have made work

A factory on wheels in the celery fields.

Harvested onions are left to cure on the black soil.

Knibbe, of the research station, explained once. "Special double wheels have to be installed on the machinery to distribute the weight more evenly. That can be costly to a farmer, because the adaptations can be expensive on various types of machinery. But if he didn't go through with this expense, he would find himself spending more time trying to pull stuck equipment out of the fields than he would actually working them."

Although their numbers are not like what they used to be, seasonal labourers are still needed. In the growing season, it's not unusual to spot them on their knees in the muck, thinning out lettuce plants, in much the same way as the pioneers had done in the '30's. In late summer and fall, most of them work with the latest machinery in getting the crops off the land.

In the early days, most of the labourers were immigrants from the Netherlands and other European countries. That's changed a lot easier for the growers. Mind you, the combines and other specialized equipment require substantial capital outlays. But they are looked upon as indispensable investments with some key benefits: they reduce the labour costs sharply and make operations such as seeding, spraying, harvesting and packaging much more efficient.

Marsh growers, by the way, must adapt every implement, from field wagon to harvester, to prevent them from getting mired in the spongy soil.

"The muck won't hold the weight of a tractor," Edo

Marsh grower Ky Chan specializes in oriental vegetable varieties.

Vegetable Crop Survey

Commodity Est.	1987	1988	1989	1990	1991
Onions	3600	3696	3746	3770	3795
Carrots	4050	3301	3370	3097	3206
Lettuce	640	798	557	504	562
Celery	585	525	519	466	409
Potatoes	300	332	375	306	378
Parsnips	50	65	121	163	97
Cabbage	60	80	61	63	37
Cauliflower	100	83	78	57	54
Beets	40	50	56	46	56
Radish	40	44	58	38	57
Romaine	200	195	210	84	123
Misc. crops	314	218	344	399	444
Total acreage	9979	9387	9495	8993	9218

These statistics include all acreage within the perimeter of the Holland Marsh canals as well as the Beeton, Colbar, Cookstown, Keswick, Mount Albert and Orillia Township marshes. Oriental vegetable varieties are included in the miscellaneous figures.

Growers Per Farm Operation in 1991

31 growers operated under 11 acres
33 growers operated 11 acres to 20 acres
15 growers operated 21 acres to 30 acres
29 growers operated 31 acres to 50 acres
18 growers operated 51 acres to 75 acres
11 growers operated 76 acres to 100 acres
17 growers operated 101 acres to 150 acres
6 growers operated 151 acres to 200 acres
9 growers operated over 200 acres

Holland Marsh counted 169 growers in 1991.

too. Now they're likely to be people from the Caribbean — farmers call them offshore help — or from Mexico. They form a reliable labour pool in a time when field workers are hard to find.

After the reclamation, the Marsh was gradually divided into small parcels, some only five acres in extent. While this enabled many people of modest means to acquire land, and thus contribute to the development of the area, there was a drawback: with such small parcels, the growers couldn't afford to rotate their crops, let the land lie fallow, or plough in a field of clover periodically, so as to replenish the fibre in the soil.

But nowadays many of the operations are much larger, and little concern is heard about the land's fertility being exhausted. With the trend to larger acreage, the number of growers is dropping, of course. In 1991 there were only 169 (see chart), a sharp decline from, say, the five hundred recorded in 1949.

Descendants of some of the pioneer families are still in the Marsh, working the land. Many of them are related by marriage; it's like one big family. But many of the old names have disappeared.

John van Dyke, the historian of sorts, whose five acres eventually grew to twenty-five, quit farming in 1966 when he was sixty years old.

"Things were changing in the Marsh at that time," he explained. "Big machinery for mechanical harvesting was coming in and the little farmers were being cleared out. My boys didn't want to follow in my footsteps, so I said to myself: 'I'm not going into all that big stuff, getting in the hole for $60-$70,000.'

Seedless cucumbers are grown in the fully computerized and automated greenhouse operation of Bob Voorberg.

Without the machinery, I would have had to continue to do much of the work by hand, and I wouldn't have been able to compete any more. So I sold out."

He and his wife, Grace, continued to live in their little house in the Marsh, and they spent many happy summers together in a trailer park near the Ontario city of Peterborough. She died of cancer in 1979. Van Dyke later married Grace's

Another truck with vegetables leaves the Marsh.

The houses built by the settlers are still in use.

Tyler Visser and his sister, Jillayna, try out the playground equipment at the park in Ansnorveldt.

cousin, Henrietta, who was born in 1913 in Chicago to Frisian-born parents. In 1986, they moved away from the Marsh, to Lethbridge, Alberta, to be closer to relatives. He died in the fall of 1992.

Although the Dutch still form a sizeable part of the Marsh's population - some say twenty-five

One of the road signs in Ansnorveldt.

A piece of equipment rumbles over a bridge spanning the canal at Ansnorveldt.

per cent, compared with forty per cent in 1961 and close to 100 per cent in the beginning - their numbers are continuing to dwindle. Large groups of people of Hungarian, German, Polish, Czechoslovakian, Ukrainian and Italian background make their living there, side by side, as well as those of many other nationalities, including Portuguese, Chinese and Japanese.

This multi-cultural aspect of the Marsh community was celebrated in late August, 1992, with the first annual Bradford West Gwillimbury Summer Festival, featuring the customs, costumes and cuisine of a number of countries. The Dutch, for example, brought in a maker of wooden shoes, dancers and even a barrel organ to give the non-Dutch a flavour of their background. The organizers of the festival were confident that the event would grow in future years, as more ethnic groups planned to become involved.

The main crops are still the same. In most years, carrots take up the biggest acreage, followed closely by onions. Next on the popularity list are lettuce, potatoes, celery, beets, radishes, spinach and so on. Recent years have seen a steady growth in crops of the Toronto specialty market, including endive, dandelion, mustard and various oriental varieties.

In the early days, the average grower depended on a variety of crops to make a profit. Should one crop fail, another one might thrive and balance the loss.

Growers nowadays are almost certain to have a good yield on any crop they plant, due mainly to better irrigation and soil preparation and the use of more efficient sowing and harvesting equipment.

Pioneer Jan Rupke had dreams of turning the Marsh into a version of Westland, an area in the province of Zuid-Holland

which is virtually covered with glass. "He was so convinced of this," said son John, "that he even had a little greenhouse of his own."

At one time, it appeared as if Rupke's grand vision was going to become reality. A number of growers launched indoor operations. Before long, there were seventeen of them, producing spring and fall tomato crops, seedless cucumbers and even commercial flowers such as orchids, roses, mums and box plants.

But the smaller concerns found it increasingly difficult to remain viable, and gradually disappeared, leaving the greenhouse business in the hands of the larger operators. At last

Alice Visser takes her grandchildren, Tyler and Jillayna, on a visit to the library in Ansnorveldt.

Holland Street, the main thoroughfare of Bradford, usually handles a lot of traffic.

count, there were nine survivors - five with flowers and four with vegetables.

Among them is Bob Voorberg who came to the Marsh in 1949 from the district - Westland - whose enterprise Rupke wanted to emulate. He acquired a ten-acre lot and embarked on outside growing. But he wasn't satisfied. He was, after all, a greenhouse man.

"After Hurricane Hazel," he recalled, "we got compensation from the government. I used the funds to get started in the greenhouse business."

He has never looked back. At first, he grew tomatoes. Now he and son Ron, who has taken over the helm, produce 1.2 million seedless cucumbers a year. The greenhouses, which cover 3 1/2 acres, are completely computerized and automated. "We are so up to date," said Voorberg, "we are having trouble thinking of what else to do. But technology has a habit of becoming obsolete."

Voorberg's initiative and foresight are exemplified in his decision to pioneer the use of a new heating system for the greenhouses, involving the burning of sawdust obtained from a manufacturer of kitchen cabinets.

"It works great for us. We burn 2,000 tons of sawdust a year and save considerably on oil and gas. But the idea has never really taken off. A rose grower here did it, and so did a few others in Ontario. You see, when we started this, everyone expected oil prices to go through the roof. But they didn't. So the incentive is not there to invest $300,000 to set up the system. In our case, government subsidies partly covered the cost. We got paid for making mistakes and introducing new technologies."

Voorberg was instrumental in the birth of the Greenhouse Vegetable Marketing Board, a price-setting organization for growers in Ontario. He had been disgruntled with the dog-eat-dog way of doing business. Now he sells his cucumbers at an established price through wholesalers in Ontario, Quebec and some parts of the U.S.

He is also an elected member of the municipal council of King Township, deeply involved in looking after the interests of the people of the Marsh and making sure that the area continues to live up to its well-deserved reputation as a big-quantity, high-quality producer.

"For those who have lived here a long time," remarked an old-timer, "the landscape has changed considerably. Just look at the greenhouses and the big storage barns. We're not standing still, that's for sure. We never have."

Time has changed Ansnorveldt too.

It isn't much bigger than it was before, which is just fine with the local authorities, as prime agricultural land is being preserved. And most of the original houses are still there. But it is not the same closely-knit community where people once lived in relative harmony and openly shared their happiness and sorrow, their cultural background and their religious beliefs. Now many of the familiar Dutch names have disappeared from the roadside mailboxes.

A few years ago, Harry van der Kooij, a resident, observed: "It appears that some of the houses are being used as starter homes. The properties change ownership quite often and are mostly lived in by younger couples and families attracted by the relatively low houses prices. The friendly neighbourhood atmosphere is no more."

Van der Kooij often reflected on the quality of life of bygone years. He'd been a resident of Ansnorveldt and vicinity ever since his father, Arie, bought one of the houses in 1949 for $2,600. With nine children in the family, there was little elbow room. And Dad made only fifty cents an hour, meaning that anything beyond the basic necessities was out of reach. Yet everyone seemed happy and satisfied. Moreover, there was a strong sense of community, undoubtedly generated by the isolation and the common interests.

"The new owners," Van der Kooij once lamented, "appear reluctant to become involved in community affairs. For example, hardly any of them show up at the well-advertised annual Ansnorveldt Park meeting."

This park is on King Township property next to the Christian school. Volunteer labour, mostly from members of the school society, was instrumental in its development. It contains a baseball diamond, a soccer field and a creative play area, as well as new playground equipment. Near the dike, a small area of the natural vegetation, including trees and dense brush, has been left in its original state. It is a favourite spot for the more adventuresome youngsters.

Nowadays Van der Kooij is not as disheartened with the state of civic pride, and community involvement, as he used to be.

"The community," he said, "appears to be stabilizing once again."

This was evidenced by the large turnout for a fund-raiser to establish a branch library of the King City Library Board in the park in 1990. This modest building of 768 square feet, whose simple style fits the architectural heritage of the Marsh perfectly, cost approximately $48,000. The township and a provincial grant covered two-thirds of the expenditures, but the remainder was the responsibility of the local community.

The people responded admirably. Even the Christian school, whose students are among the regular borrowers, presented a $3,000 cheque.

Of course, there is still apathy, and aloofness, which can be excused as a sign of the times. Things do change. They have ever since people first moved to the Marsh to eke out a living.

Why, even Bradford is not a separate entity any more. It amalgamated with West Gwillimbury Township on January 1, 1991, forming the town of Bradford West Gwillimbury, with a combined population of about seventeen thousand.

Happily, there are a few things which have stayed the same over the years. A local chronicler has recorded: "The only things which have not changed in the valley in more than half a century are the rich, black organic soil, the air, which still hangs heavy with the rising morning mist in the spring and fall, and the unmistakable, pungent aroma of onions in the summer."

By the way, an acre of this onion land these days is worth between $12,000 and $15,000, depending on the depth of the muck, availability of water for irrigation, and location.

~~~

Bibliography

Much of the information used in this history was assembled through interviews with people directly involved in the development of the Marsh. The following literature was also very helpful:

Anniversary Book,
Holland Marsh District Christian School, 1943-1983.

25th Anniversary Commemorative Book,
Springdale Christian Reformed Church, 1952-1977.

35th Anniversary Album and Directory,
Springdale Christian Reformed Church, 1952-1987.

50 Years CRC in Chatham,
by Ray Koning, 1976.

Anniversary Book,
Holland Marsh Christian Reformed Church, 1978.

A Bittersweet Land, the Dutch Experience in Canada 1890-1980,
by Herman Ganzevoort,
published by McClalland and Stewart, 1988.

Bradford's 125th Anniversary,
edited by John Slykhuis, 1982.

Bradford, 100 years in picture and story,
compiled and arranged by the *Bradford Witness*, 1957.

The Bradford Witness,
a weekly newspaper whose editors, Stewart and Ina McKenzie, gave thorough coverage to events on the Marsh.

Canada,
by G.W.N. van der Sleen, published by Nederland's Boekhuis, 1947.

Canada, een Jonge Reus Onder de Landen,
by J.J. van der Laan,
published in the 1950's by Uitgeversmaatschappij Holland.

Canada, een Land met Grote Mogelijkheden,
by S.J. Hovius and T. Plomp, published by J. Niemeijer, 1950.

Canada, Land van Vrijheid, Ruimte en Ontplooiing,
by T. Cnossen,
director of the Centrale Stichting Landbouw Emigratie,
published by Zomer en Keuning, the Netherland, in the 1950's.

Canada, Reis met Onbekende Bestemming,
by J.W. Hofwijk,
published by N.V. Uitgevers De Lanteern, 1952-53.

Canada Calling,
written by H.G. de Maar and E.W.J. de Maar and published by Erven P. Noordhoff, Groningen, the Netherlands.

De Canadezen en hun land,
by W.G.N. van der Sleen,
published by Nederland's Boekhuis in 1952.

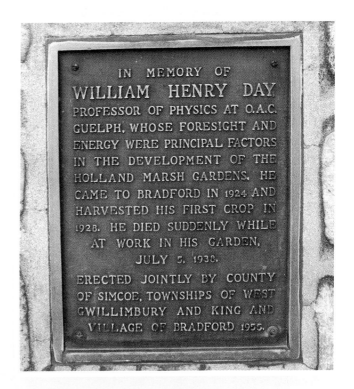

Cauliflower Crown,
by Klaas de Jong, who came to Canada in 1893 and won recognition as a top market gardener, published by Western Producer Book Service, 1973.

A Dutch Homesteader on the Prairies,
by Willem de Gelder, University of Toronto Press, 1973.

Of Dutch Ways,
an insighful look at the Netherlands and its people,
by Helen Colijn, published by Dillon Press Inc., 1980.

Early Settlements of King Township,
The University of Toronto Press, 1984.

Family, Kinship and Community,
a study of the Dutch community in Holland Marsh
by Dr. Karigouder Ishwaran, McGraw-Hill Ryerson, 1977.

Fifty Years, anniversary book of First Hamilton Christian Reformed Church, 1979.

De Gids Voor Emigranten Naar Canada,
an information guide for prospective immigrants from the Netherlands, published by the Christian Reformed Church, 1947.

Historical Sketches of Ontario,
Ontario Ministry of Culture and Recreation, 1976.

Holland Marsh Gardens,
Trade and Transportation,
published by A. H. Wilford and Associates, Toronto, 1949.

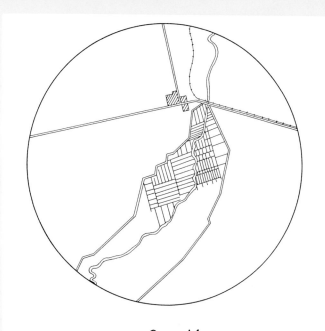

OLD MARSH

PATTERN OF LAND HOLDINGS
AND DRAINAGE DITCHES

Holland Marsh Gives Wonderful Results,
report by Prof. William Day to the townships of King and West
Gwillimbury, 1930.

The Holland Marsh,
script for slide set produced by the Ontario Ministry of Agriculture
and Food.

Hollanders in Canada,
by K. Norel,
published by A. Roelofs in the Netherlands in the 1950's.

Hurricane Hazel,
part of a series of articles written by Edo Knibbe for the 40th anniversary of the Springdale Christian Reformed Church, 1992.

Klein Nederland in het hart van Canada,
article in Wereldkroniek, an illustrated weekly published in The
Hague, June 8, 1946.

Land voor onze zonen,
an account of the experiences of an immigrant in Canada, by Maxine
Brandis, published by Prisma-Boeken, 1960.

The Life and Times of Samuel Holland,
by W. Chipman, the Ontario Historical Society, 1924.

Life in the Muck,
article in the magazine Equinox, May/June, 1990.

Living in a New Country,
by T.C. Van Kooten,
Guardian Publishing, Hamilton, Ontario, 1959.

Management of Organic Soils,
fact sheet of the Ontario
Ministry of Agriculture and Food, Matthew Valk, 1980.

Mission Work of Our Denomination,
article in The Banner, Dr. Henry Beets, 1935.

The Netherlands,
a history book for travellers, Thames and Hudson, 1972.

News Release,
Ontario Heritage Foundation, 1978.

A *Quarter Century in a New Land,*
publication of Classis Hamilton of the
Christian Reformed Church, 1977.

Reclamation of Holland Marsh,
article by W.H. Day in The Canadian Engineer, 1927.

Report of the Committee Appointed for a Drainage Engineering
Study of the Holland Marsh Area, 1967.

Samuel Holland, Canada's First Surveyor General,
by Janny Lowenstein, Canadian Journal of Netherlandic Studies,
The Windmill Herald.

The Strenght of Their Years,
by Tymen E. Hofman, Knight Publishing Limited,
St. Catharines, Ontario, 1983.

A Study of Holland Marsh,
Its Reclamation and Development,
published by the Immigration Branch of the Ontario Department of
Planning and Development, 1949.

To All Our Children,
a history of the postwar Dutch immigration to Canada,
Paideia Press, 1983.

Toiling and Trusting,
address by S.A. Winter, 1963.

Van de Canadeesche Velden,
a series of newspaper articles for Het Nieuwsblad van het Noorden
by J. Aberson (nee Uges), and republished in two volumes by Erven
A. de Jager, Groningen, 1933.

Water Management Plan for the Holland Marsh,
V.G. Bardawill and A.E. Berry, 1970.

When Through Fiery Trial,
research paper, Marge Pott, 1983.

The Windmill Herald,
a Dutch-Canadian bi-weekly, which has published extensive ac-
counts of the Dutch role in reclamation works in a number of countries over the centuries. The paper features articles on the Dutch in
North America on a regular basis.

~~~

Index

~~~

Registries

Prepublication Registry

The publishers acknowledge the keen interest and support by many in the community who ordered a copy of the book when it was still in the early preparatory stage. We offer our sincere apologies for any omissions from this list.

Robert Anes, Brantford, ON
H. Baarda, Smithville, ON
Evelyn Baker, Georgetown, ON
P.H. Barnsley, Assiniboia, SK
Nicolaas Beers, Merritt, BC
Maria Benjamins, Covina, CA
M. Bartels, Fonthill, ON
Maria Bergs, Willowdale, ON
Henry Bisschop, Chilliwack, BC
C. Blanken, Caledonia, ON
John L. Boot, Scotland, ON
Mrs. Eleanor Both, Shallow Lake, ON
Nelly Brands-Rupke, Brampton, ON
Brenda Bos, Holland, MI
Mrs. J. Bremer, Bobcaygeon, ON
Eric Brouwer, Queensville, ON
Peter Brouwer, Kettleby, ON
K. Cor Brouwers, Pella, IA
Kornelis Buikema, Georgetown, ON
Hans Burgers, Scarborough, ON
Mrs. D. Bylsma, Whitby, ON
Francina Carter, LeHigh Acres, FL
Dick Coers, Welland, ON
H. Cillessen, Guelph, ON
Mrs. Linda Cripps-Verkaik, Eustis, FL
W. (Lee) Dam, Vernon, BC
Sybren de Boer, Exeter, ON
Klaas De Jong, Hamilton, ON
H. De Haan, Weston, ON
J. Eisen family, 1949-1956, ON
James and Ellen Eisse, Debert, NS

———

Auke Ellens, Bradford, On
Cornelius Radder, 1948-1963
Leon Radder, 1963-1992
Christian Radder, 1948-1956
Norman Knibbe (since 1980)

———

George and Gerda Engelage, Murillo, ON
H. Engelage, Whitby, ON
Sophie Ensing, Victoria, BC
Johannes H. Evertman, Toronto, ON
H. Fennema, Langley, BC
Dr. G. H. Gerrits, Coldbrook, NS
Inze Graanstra, Duncan, BC
Bert Hanemaayer, Kettleby, ON
Peter and Wilma Hanemaayer & Family, Kettleby, ON
Jacob Harfman, Kelowna, BC
Holland Marsh District, New Market, ON
Geert Horinga, Port Colborne, ON

———

Walter, Hettie Horlings and Family 1935-1967
Al, Katriena Verrips and Family 1936-1982

Walter and Hettie Horlings Sr. and Family:
Joan Horlings - Peter Schaafsma
Tom Horlings - Helen Verrips
Elsie Horlings, Thornhill, ON
Frank Horlings - Betty-Ann Foran
Walter Horlings Jr. - Nance Schrotenboer

———

John Houweling, Wyoming, MI
John Kapteyn, Phelpston, ON
George Keep and Family, Brampton, ON
E. J. Klein-Horsman, Cedar Valley, ON
Wilma Kleine, Richmond Hill, ON
Dinah Koot, St. Pauls, ON
J. Kraayenbrink, Ingersoll, ON
Nicholas C. and Ruth Kramer, Zeeland, MI
J. George Lantrok, Owen Sound, ON
Trudy Lieverse, Beaver Lodge, AB
Mrs. Anna Luke (nee Posthumus), Scarborough, ON
Dijkje Luijt, Los Angeles, CA
Marinus C. Mol, Ayton, ON
Arie Moor and Family, Kettleby, ON (since 1952)
Nan Mulder, Portage Prairie, MB
Newmarket Public Library, Newmarket, ON
Richard Oostra, Calgary, AB
Rose Philip, London, ON
John Plat, Drayton, ON
Mrs. G. Pluim, Kitchener, ON
Titus Porcee, Barrie, ON
Donald Post, Brampton, ON
Bob and Ann Postma, Sarnia, ON
G. J. Rhebergen and Family, Totenham, ON
John Rupke, Kettleby, ON
Jack Rupke and Sons Ltd, Kettleby, ON (since 1967)
Nel Sanchez, Mountain View, CA
Bert Schapelhouman, Mountain View, CA
Berend Scholten, Orangeville, ON
F. J. Schryer, Kitchener, ON
Henry Shotmeyer, Franklin Lakes, NJ
Mrs. Elsey H. M. Sneep, Chatham, ON

———

Maria Koot (Snor), daughter of
John J. Snor 1910-1992

Grandchildren:
Michael John Kott
Susan Cornelia Swayze
Catherine Jane Darling
Thomas Charles Kott
Timothy Karl Kott

Great grandchildren:
Gary Joel Swayze

Janet Elizabeth Knight
John Timothy Kott
Michael Gordon Kott
Gregory Charles Kott
Ryan Matthew Kott
Andrew Joseph Kott
Jeremy Thomas Kott

———

St. Charles School, Bradford, ON
H. Storteboom, Brampton, ON
George and Ada Struyk, Cochrane, ON
Helen Sutton, Dorset, ON
Harold Sutton, Huntsville, ON
Andy te Nyenhuis, Oro Station, ON
Ralph Tevelde, Utopia, ON
A. Tillema, Calgary, AB
Glen Tilstra, Dunnville, ON
William G. Turkenburg, Grand Rapids, MI
Marinus P. Van Brugge, Kalamazoo, MI
Andrew A. Vanden Berg, Walkerton, ON
John Van den Elzen, Allentown, PA
Ted Vander Goot, Bradford, ON
Arie Vander Kooij, 1954-1968
Peter Vander Kooij, 1962-1964
Harry Vander Kooij, Newmarket, ON
Leni Vander Kooij, Bradford, ON
Gerrit Vander Mark, Coaticook, PQ
Catherine Vander Veen, Brantford, ON
Johanna Vander Veen, Wyoming, MI
Geo Vander Vecht, Woodstock, ON
Maarten and Jennie Van Driel (nee Tenhage), Delta, BC
Prof. Harry Van Dyke, Ancaster, ON
Peter Van Dyken, Newmarket, ON (since 1954)
Jacobus (Koos) Van Hemert 1947-1982
Rev. John and Jean Van Hemert (nee Tenhage), Lantana, FL
H. Van Leeuwaarden, Montreal, PQ
Adrian Van Luyk Sr., Newmarket, ON
Adrianus (Jack) Van Luyk 1934-1967
Douglas James Van Luyk (since 1986)
A. H. Van Mansum, Ottawa, ON
A. Van Nieuwburg, Beaconsfield, PQ
Pete Van Reeuwyk, Campbell River, BC
B. G. Van't Spyker, Alliston, ON
Sara Veenstra, Smithers, BC
Pieter Velthove, Norwich, ON
Arend J. Veltkamp, Kincardine, ON
Bram Verhoeff, Toronto, ON
John Verkaik, Eustis, FL
Peter Verkaik, Eustis, FL
Martin Verkuyl, Woodstock, ON
N. Vink, Windsor, ON
Brian J. and Theresa Visser, Kettleby, ON
John Vooys, Surrey, BC
Bob Voorberg, Kettleby, ON
J. Vreugdenhil, Moraga, CA
P. Vriezema, Barrie, ON
Frank Wassenaar, Lacombe, AB
Gerda Weamire, Whittier, AK
T. Werkman, Mission, BC

Mrs. Mary Wesseluis, Brandon, MB
G.B. Wikkerink, Cobble Hill, BC
Charles Wiersma, Waupun, WI

Farmers' Registry

Listings were voluntarily submitted and represent a small segment of the hundreds of who (co)farmed in the Marsh. Efforts to locate lists proved to be unsuccesful.

H. Baarda, Smithville, ON
Nelly Brands-Rupke, Brampton, ON
Peter Brouwer, Kettleby, ON
Mrs. Linda Cripps (Verkaik), Eustis, FL
J. Eisen family, 1949-1956
George and Gerda Englage, Murillo, ON
Annette Hanemaayer, 1947-1957, Springdale, ON
Bert Hanemaayer, Kettleby, ON
Peter and Wilma Hanemaayer and Family (since 1962)
Walter, Hettie Horlings and Family 1935-1967
John Houweling, Wyoming, MI
George Keep and Family, Brampton, ON
Wilma Klein, Richmond Hill, ON
Norman Knibbe (since 1980)
Mrs. Anna Luke (nee Posthumus), Scarborough, ON
Arie Moor and Family (since 1952), Kettleby, ON
Christian Radder 1948-1956
Cornelius Radder 1948-1963
Leon Radder 1963-1992
Gerald J. Rhebergen and Family, Tottenham, ON
Jack Rupke, Kettleby, ON
John Rupke, Kettleby, ON
Bert Schapelhouman, Mountain View, CA
Mrs. Elsey H. M. Sneep, Chatham, ON
Mrs. Helen Sutton, Dorset, ON
G. Tenhage
John Vanden Elzen, Allentown, PA
Ted Vander Goot, Bradford, ON
Arie Vander Kooij 1954-1968
Harry Vander Kooij, Newmarket, ON
Peter Vander Kooij 1962-1964
Marinus Van Dyken
Peter Van Dyken, Newmarket, ON (since 1954)
J. Van Hemert, Holland Marsh
Jacobus (Koos) Van Hemert 1947-1982
H. Van Leeuwaarden, Montreal, PQ
Adrianus (Jack) Van Luyk, 1934-1967
Adrian Van Luyk (since 1964)
Douglas James Van Luyk (since 1986)
A. H. Van Mansum, Ottawa, ON
John Verkaik, Eustis, FL
Peter Verkaik, Eustis, FL
Martin Verkuyl, Woodstock, ON
Al, Katriena Verrips & family 1936-1967
Brian J. and Theresa Visser, Kettleby, ON
Bob Voorberg, Kettleby, ON

~~~

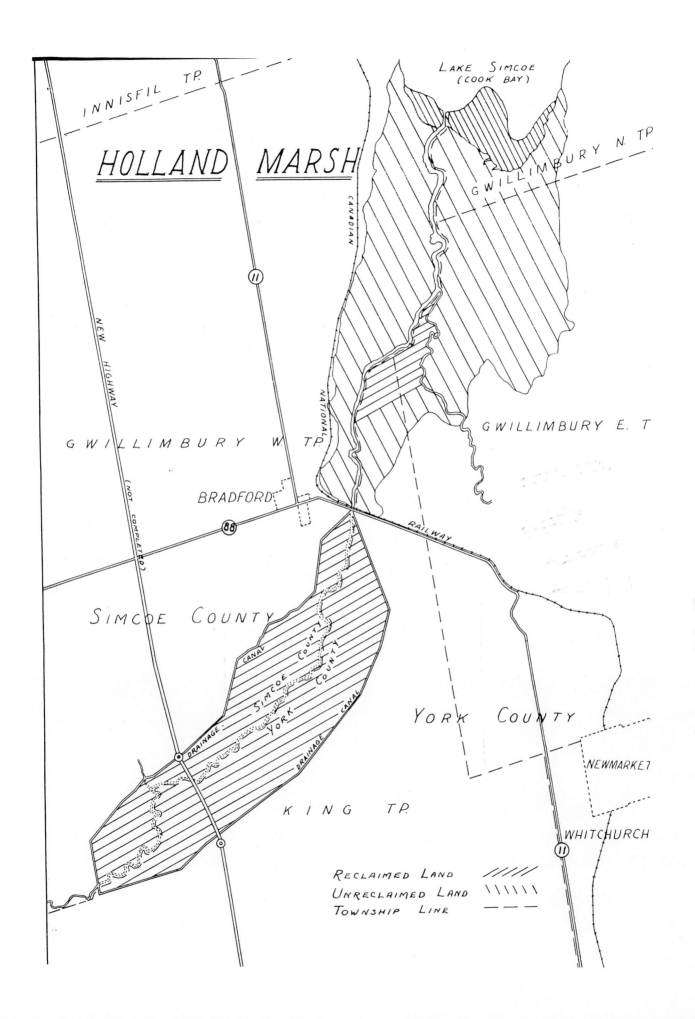

HOLLAND MARSH

INNISFIL TP.

LAKE SIMCOE
(COOK BAY)

GWILLIMBURY N. TP

GWILLIMBURY W. TP

NEW HIGHWAY (NOT COMPLETED)

CANADIAN

NATIONAL

GWILLIMBURY E. T

BRADFORD

88

RAILWAY

SIMCOE COUNTY

CANAL

DRAINAGE

Simcoe County

York County

DRAINAGE CANAL

YORK COUNTY

NEWMARKET

KING TP.

WHITCHURCH

11

RECLAIMED LAND   / / / / /
UNRECLAIMED LAND   \ \ \ \ \
TOWNSHIP LINE   — — —